Glossary and Tables for Statistical Quality Control

Also available from ASQC Quality Press

Statistical Process Control Methods for Long and Short Runs,
Second Edition
Gary K. Griffith

SPC Tools for Everyone
John T. Burr

SPC for Practitioners: Special Cases and Continuous Processes
Gary Fellers, Ph.D

Quality Control for Operators and Foremen
K.S. Krishnamoorthi

To request a complimentary catalog of publication, call 800-248-1946.

Glossary and Tables for Statistical Quality Control

Third Edition

ASQC Statistics Division

ASQC Quality Press
Milwaukee, Wisconsin

Glossary and Tables for Statistical Quality Control, Third Edition
ASQC Statistics Division

Library of Congress Cataloging-in-Publication Data

Glossary and tables for statistical quality control / ASQC Statistics
    Division. — 3rd ed.
        p. cm.
    Includes bibliographical references.
    ISBN 0-87389-354-9 (alk. paper)
    1. Quality control—Statistical methods—Terminology. 2. Quality
control—Statistical methods—Tables. I. American Society for
Quality Control. Statistics Division.
TS156.A1G53 1996
658.5′621′015195—dc20   95-51233
                                                                  CIP

10 9 8 7 6 5 4 3 2 1

ISBN 0-87389-354-9

Acquisitions Editor: Susan Westergard
Project Editor: Kelley Cardinal

ASQC Mission: To facilitate continuous improvement and increase customer sat-
isfaction by identifying, communicating, and promoting the use of quality principles, concepts, and technologies; and thereby be recognized throughout the world
as the leading authority on, and champion for, quality.

Attention: Schools and Corporations
ASQC Quality Press books, audiotapes, videotapes, and software are available at
quantity discounts with bulk purchases for business, educational, or instructional
use. For information, please contact ASQC Quality Press at 800-248-1946, or write
to ASQC Quality Press, P.O. Box 3005, Milwaukee, WI 53201-3005.

For a free copy of the ASQC Quality Press Publications Catalog, including ASQC
membership information, call 800-248-1946.

Printed in the United States of America on acid-free recycled paper.

 ASQC
Quality Press
611 East Wisconsin Avenue
Milwaukee, Wisconsin 53202

Contents

Preface

This edition is different from its predecessors in that the glossary is presented in alphabetical order. The aim of this change is to make it easier to find items of interest. Of course, other changes were made as well. Despite our best efforts to produce an updated and complete glossary, the possibility exists, of course, that something has been overlooked. Perhaps future teams will continue to improve the glossary in future editions.

As with prior editions, this glossary was compiled by a group of people dedicated to providing the best possible product. Hours were spent reviewing different definitions. It was an important, but laborious, job. I am proud of what this team accomplished, despite many setbacks along the way. I want to thank John Hromi, Ed Schilling, John Burr, and George Vorhauer for their patience and encouragement. Tom Kubiak and Joe Voelkel also provided guidance and encouragement. There were many people who offered suggestions on what should be included in this edition. We listened to all ideas and included those appropriate to our charter.

The definitions used in this glossary have been derived from the following sources. The number identifying the source follows each glossary definition.

1. ANSI/ASQC A1-1978, *Definitions, Symbols, Formulas, and Tables for Control Charts* (Milwaukee, Wis.: American Society for Quality Control, 1978).

2. ANSI/ASQC A2-1978, *Terms, Symbols, and Definitions for Acceptance Sampling* (Milwaukee, Wis.: American Society for Quality Control, 1978).

3. ANSI/ASQC A3-1978, *Quality Systems Terminology* (Milwaukee, Wis.: American Society for Quality Control, 1978).

4. ASTM Committee E-11 proposed revision to ASTM E456-72, *Terminology for Statistical Methods* (Philadelphia, Pa.: American Society for Testing and Materials, 1972).

5. ISO Technical Committee TC/69 work dealing with the *Definitions for the Design of Experiments.*

6. Terms carried over from the first edition of *Glossary and Tables for Statistical Quality Control* (Milwaukee, Wis.: ASQC Quality Press, 1973).

7. ASQC's *Journal of Quality Technology.*

8. ASQC Chemical and Process Industries Division, Chemical Interest Committee, *Quality Assurance for the Chemical and Process Industries: A Manual of Good Practices* (Milwaukee, Wis.: ASQC Quality Press, 1987).

9. T. Barker, *Engineering Quality by Design* (New York: Marcel Dekker and Milwaukee, Wis.: ASQC Quality Press, 1990).

Serving as editor was challenging and interesting. I was amazed at the number of people who were interested in the glossary's progress. I had the pleasure of making new friends and working with them at a level that few people get to experience. I hope that this glossary is beneficial to all who use it.

James L. Bossert
Editor

A

α **1:** The maximum probability, or risk, of making a type I error.

    2: The probability or risk of incorrectly deciding that a shift in process level has occurred when the process is still located at $\overline{X}_0$. (1)

acceptable process level (APL)   The process level that forms the outer boundary of the zone of acceptable processes. (A process located at the APL will have only a probability of rejection designated α when the plotted statistical measure is compared to the acceptance control limits.) (1)

Note: In the case of two-sided tolerances, upper and lower acceptable process levels will be designated UAPL and LAPL. (These need not be symmetrical around the standard level.)

acceptable process zone   See *zone of acceptable processes.* (1)

acceptable quality level (AQL)   The maximum percentage or proportion of variant units in a lot or batch that, for the purposes of acceptance sampling, can be considered satisfactory as a process average.

    The term *variant unit* should be replaced by more specific terms such as *nonconforming unit* or *defective unit,* where appropriate. (2)

1

Note: When a consumer designates some specific value of AQL for a certain characteristic or group of characteristics, the supplier is informed that the consumer's acceptance sampling plan will accept the great majority of similarly produced lots submitted by the supplier, provided that the process average for these lots, in terms of percentage of variant units, is no greater than the designated value of AQL. In this sense the AQL serves as an index for acceptance sampling plans.

The AQL alone does not describe the protection to the consumer for individual lots, but is more directly related to what might be expected from a series of lots, provided the steps called for in the referenced AQL system of procedures are taken. It is necessary to refer to the operating characteristic (OC) curve of the sampling plan that the consumer will use, or to the average outgoing quality limit (AOQL) of the plan, to determine what protection the consumer will have.

The use of percentage of variant units as an indication of quality creates the dilemma that a high percentage reflects poorer (or lower) quality and a low percentage reflects better (or higher) quality, which is contrary to common expectations of an index. However, this customary usage among quality engineers is based on the desire to have a sensitive index that calls attention to areas that need it. On the other hand, there are times when it seems more appropriate to discuss the percentage of normal units rather than percentage of variant units. From a quality engineering viewpoint, this often has the disadvantage of appearing relatively unreflective of shifts in quality level, but for some purposes it may be more meaningful.

acceptance (control chart or acceptance control chart usage)

A decision that the process is operating in a satisfactory manner with respect to the statistical measure being plotted. (1)

acceptance control chart

A graphical method for the dual purposes of evaluating a process in terms of (a) whether or not it can be expected to satisfy product or service tolerances for the characteristic(s) being measured and (b) whether or not it is in a state of statistical control with respect to within-sample, or subgroup, variability. (The determinations are made through comparison of values of some statistical measure(s) for an ordered series of samples, or subgroups, with acceptance control limits.) (1)

Note:

The emphasis of the acceptance control chart, as contrasted to the control chart, is that the process usually does not need to remain in control about some single standard process level. As long as the within-subgroup variability remains in control, it can run at any level or levels within some zone of process levels that would be acceptable in terms of tolerance requirements. It is assumed that some assignable causes will create shifts in the process level that are small enough in relation to requirements that it would not be economically feasible to attempt to control them too tightly.

The regular acceptance control chart, as contrasted to the modified control chart (or control chart with modified limits), also considers the probabilities (risks) of failing to detect process shifts of some specified magnitude as well as the probabilities (risks) of incorrectly signaling a shift from the standard or acceptable process zone levels, and permits determination of the appropriate sample size to maintain these risks at desired levels. A state of statistical control with respect to within-subgroup variability is important in assuring inherent process stability, and the term *acceptance control chart* implies the use of a control chart for ranges or a control chart for sample standard deviation. Acceptance control chart limits are shown in Figure 1. The following table displays formulas for acceptance control charts.

Acceptable process levels:	$\text{UAPL} = \text{UTL} - z_{p1}\sigma$
	$\text{LAPL} = \text{LTL} + z_{p1}\sigma$
Rejectable process levels:	$\text{URPL} = \text{UTL} - z_{p2}\sigma$
	$\text{LRPL} = \text{LTL} + z_{p2}\sigma$
Acceptance control limits:	$\text{UACL} = \text{UAPL} + z_{\alpha}\sigma/\sqrt{n}$
	$\text{LACL} = \text{LAPL} - z_{\alpha}\sigma/\sqrt{n}$
	or
	$\text{UACL} = \text{URPL} - z_{\beta}\sigma/\sqrt{n}$
	$\text{LACL} = \text{LRPL} + z_{\beta}\sigma/\sqrt{n}$

Sample size:
$$n = [(z_{\alpha} + z_{\beta})\sigma/(\text{RPL} - \text{APL})]^2$$

Note: If *n* is not an integer, use the nearest integer and recompute the α and β values or modify the APL and RPL definitions.

acceptance control limit (ACL) The action criterion for an acceptance control chart. (A point plotting outside the ACL indicates that the process is operating at an undesirable level.) (1)

Note: Because most tolerances are two-sided, there usually will be both upper and lower accep-

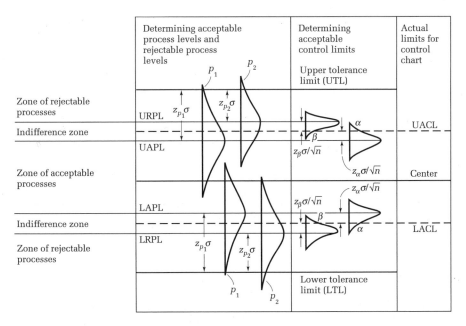

Figure 1. Acceptance control chart limits.

tance control limits (UACL and LACL). These need not be symmetrical around the standard level, as the criteria for determining the location of the limit (such as the APL, RPL, or desired risks of error) may differ for processes located above or below the standard level.

acceptance number (attributes)

The maximum number of variants or variant units in the sample that will permit acceptance of the inspected lot or batch. (2)

Note:

The term *variant* should be replaced by more specific terms such as *nonconformity* and *defect*, where appropriate. The term *variant unit* should be replaced by more specific terms such as *nonconforming unit* and *defective unit*, where appropriate.

acceptance sampling

Sampling inspection in which decisions are made to accept or not accept product or service;

also, the methodology that deals with procedures by which decisions to accept or not accept are based on the results of the inspection of samples. (2)

Note: The alternative to acceptance often is termed *rejection*, although in practice the alternative may take some form other than outright rejection. See also note under *reject*.

In lot-by-lot sampling, acceptance and nonacceptance relate to individual lots. In continuous sampling, acceptance and nonacceptance relate to individual units or to blocks of consecutive units, depending on the stated procedure.

acceptance sampling plan A specific plan that states the sample size or sizes to be used, and the associated acceptance and nonacceptance criteria. (2)

acceptance sampling scheme A specific set of procedures, which usually consists of acceptance sampling plans, in which lot sizes, sample sizes, and acceptance criteria, or the amount of 100 percent inspection and sampling, are related. Schemes typically contain rules for switching from one plan to another. (2)

acceptance sampling system A collection of sampling schemes. (6)

accuracy The closeness of agreement between an observed value and an accepted reference value.

Note: The term *accuracy*, when applied to a set of observed values, will be a combination of a random component and a common systematic error or bias component. Because in routine application random components and bias components cannot be completely separated, the reported accuracy must be interpreted as a combination of these two elements. The use of the terms *imprecision* to describe random errors and *bias* to describe systematic errors will emphasize these distinct elements of variation. When assessing the systematic error (bias) of test methods or operations, use of the term *bias* will avoid confusion. See also *bias*, *precision*, and *uncertainty*. (4)

action limits   See *control limits*. (1)

adaptive control chart   A control chart that provides information for controlling a process by evaluating predicted values based on current data for the process and quantifying the adjustment needed to avoid undesirable deviations from the specified standard level. (1)

Note: This technique applies to those situations in which process adjustments can be made readily in terms of cost and ease of adjustment, and in which the need for tight adherence to the standard level is important. It involves the use of prediction models of varying degrees of complexity to anticipate where the process will be if left to continue as it is currently operating, and taking prompt corrective action to prevent the process from departing from the standard level.

The word *control* for this type of chart is used in the sense of actively directing a change in the process, whereas in the control chart and acceptance control chart, the word *control* refers to a state of statistical stability or constancy of the cause system.

aliases   Two or more effects (main or interaction) in a fractional factorial experiment that are estimated by the same contrast and, therefore, cannot be estimated separately. (5)

Notes: 1. The determination of which effects in a
2^n factorial are aliased can be made once the
defining contrast (in the case of half replicate) or
defining contrasts (for a fraction smaller than ½)
are stated. The defining contrast is that effect (or
effects), usually thought to be of no conse-
quence, about which all information may be
sacrificed for the experiment. An identity I is
equated to the defining contrast (or defining
contrasts), and, using the convention that $A^2 =
B^2 = C^2 = D = I$, the multiplication of the letters
on both sides of the equation shows the aliases.

In the example given in the fractional factorial design definition,

$$I = ABCD$$

so that

$$A = A^2BCD = BCD$$

and

$$AB = A^2B^2CD = CD.$$

2. With a large number of factors (and factorial treatment combinations) the size of the
experiment can be reduced to ¼, ⅓ or in general
to $½^k$ to form a 2^{n-k} fractional factorial.

3. There exist generalizations of the above
to factorials having more than two levels.

alternative   The hypothesis that is accepted if the null hy-
hypothesis (H_1)   pothesis is disproved. The choice of alternative
hypothesis will determine whether one-tail or
two-tail tests are applicable. (6)

analysis of   A technique for estimating and testing the ef-
covariance   fects of treatments when one or more concom-

itant variables influence the response variable. (5)

Note: Usually the concomitant variable cannot be accounted for in the design of the experiment and its undesirable effect on the results must then be taken into account in the analysis. For example, the experimental units for which the versions of the selected factors have been set may differ in the amount of some chemical constituent present in each unit that is varying concurrently, but independently, and that can be measured, but not adjusted.

Example: Because of the concomitant variable X_c, an analysis of variance may produce biased results. The assumed model for a single-factor analysis of variance ordinarily would be $Y_{est_{ij}} = \mu_j$. To account for the contribution of the concomitant variable, the model might become $Y_{est_{ij}} + B(X_{cj} - X_c)$. A regression analysis could be used to obtain B by pooling the within-version value for $\sum X^2_{cij}$ and $\sum X_{cij}Y_{ij}$ with $B = \sum X_{cij}Y_{ij}/\sum X^2_{cij}$. The Y values could then be adjusted to account for the X_c values.

analysis of variance (ANOVA) A technique that subdivides the total variation of a set of data into meaningful component parts associated with specific sources of variation for the purpose of testing some hypothesis on the parameters of the model or estimating variance components.

An analysis of variance table usually contains columns for

1. Source of variation
2. Sum of squares (SS)
3. Degrees of freedom (DF) (analogous to the denominator $n - 1$ in the definition of sample variance s^2)

4. Mean square (MS) (the sum of squares divided by the degrees of freedom)

Another column, "Expected mean square," is often added to serve as a guide showing which mean squares under the assumed model are to be compared in an F test. When the versions (levels) are selected at random, the expected mean squares show the composition of the components of variance assignable to the appropriate sources. See also *model II analysis of variance*. (5)

Example: In a *randomized block design*, the observation obtained from the ith of t treatments in the jth of r blocks is denoted by Y_{ij} ($i = 1, 2, \ldots, t$; $j = 1, 2, \ldots, r$). Then, the following ANOVA table is computed, where $S_T = S_A + S_B + S_e$ and $V_T = V_A + V_B + V_e$ hold.

Source	SS	DF
Total	$S_T = \Sigma_i\Sigma_j(Y_{ij} - Y_{..})^2$	$v_T = rt - 1$
Treatment	$S_A = r\Sigma_i(Y_{ij} - Y_{i.})^2$	$v_A = t - 1$
Block	$S_B = t\Sigma_i(Y_{ij} + Y_{.j})^2$	$v_b = r - 1$
Error	$S_e = \Sigma_i\Sigma_j(U_{ij} - Y_{i.} - Y_{.j} + Y_{..})^2$	$v_e = (t - 1)(r - 1)$

MS	F	E[MS]
$MS_A = S_A/V_A$	$F_{vA,ve} = MS_A/MS_e$	$\sigma^2 + rk^2_A$
$MS_B = S_B/V_B$	$F_{vB,ve} = MS_B/MS_e$	$\sigma^2 + tk^2_B$
$MS_e = S_e/V_e$		σ^2

If the model associated with the observations is given as

$$Y_{ij} = \mu + \alpha_i + \beta_j + e_{ij};$$
$$i = 1, 2, \ldots, t;$$
$$j = 1, 2, \ldots, r;$$

$$\Sigma\alpha_i = \Sigma\beta_j = 0,\ e_{ij} \sim N(0,\ \sigma_2);$$

$$k_A^2 = \Sigma\alpha_1^2 / (t - 1),\ k_B^2 = \Sigma\beta_j^2 / (r - 1);$$

where μ, α_i, β_j, and e_{ij} represent the general mean, the effect of the ith treatment, the effect of the jth block, and the experimental error, respectively, the estimates of μ, α_i, β_j, and σ^2 are obtained as follows.

$$\mu_{est} = Y_{..}$$
$$\alpha_{est_1} = Y_{i.} - Y_{..}$$
$$\beta_j = Y_{.j} - Y_{..}$$
$$\sigma_{est}^2 = \Sigma\Sigma(Y_{ij} - Y_{i.} - Y_{.j} + Y_{..})^2 / \{(t - 1)(r - 1)\}$$
$$= s_e^2$$

Fv_1,v_2 is the F-statistic

Traditionally, X has been used to represent the response value in analysis of variance computations while Y is used in regression analysis and contrast analysis. Many newer textbooks are now using Y.

The simple formulas shown in the example depend upon having equal numbers of observations in the cells of the randomized block design.

Note: Basic assumptions are that the effects due to all the sources of variation are additive and that the experimental errors are independently and normally distributed with zero mean and have equal variances (homoscedasticity) throughout all subdivisions of the data. The technique, in conjunction with the F ratio, is used to provide a test of significance for the effects of these sources of variation and/or to obtain estimates of the variances attributable to these sources. The assumption of a normal distribution is required only for this test of significance and confidence intervals. Averages and interactions are usually looked at by summarizing in 2-way (or k-way) tables. This example assumes a model I fixed model.

area of opportunity

A unit or portion of a material, process, product, or service in which designated event(s) may occur. (1)

Note:

The term *area of opportunity* is often used when there is no natural unit. It may represent, for example, an area of space, an interval of time, a production item, or a final manufactured product composed of many parts. However, because this effectively serves the role of defining the unit, it is usually preferable to use the term *unit* rather than *area of opportunity*.

arithmetic mean and arithmetic average (μ—population mean)

The population estimate is given in the following formulas.

$$\mu_{est} = \overline{X}$$
$$\mu_{est} = \overline{Y}$$

μ (Greek lowercase letter mu) represents the population mean, ^ stands for "estimate of" and Σ denotes "sum of." Sometimes $\overline{X}$ or $\overline{X}_0$ (or $\overline{Y}$ or $\overline{Y}_0$ is used instead of μ.

arithmetic mean and arithmetic average ($\overline{X}$ or $\overline{Y}$—sample average)

A measure of central tendency or location that is the sum of the observations divided by the number of observations. (1)
 $\overline{X}$ and $\overline{Y}$ are computed with the following formulas.

$$\overline{X} = (\Sigma X_i)/n$$
$$\overline{Y} = (\Sigma Y_i)/n$$

Note:

There are several averages such as the arithmetic average, geometric average, and so on.

The term *average*, without any descriptor, is ordinarily the *arithmetic average*. It serves as an estimator of the center level of a process.

assignable cause   A factor that contributes to variation and that is feasible to detect and identify. (1)

assumed model   An equation that is intended to provide a functional description of the sources of information that may be obtained from an experiment. (5)

Note: The assumed model will include a term for each potential assignable cause deemed of interest in the experiment, including the factors selected for study, combinations of these factors [to represent second- or higher-order effects such as curvature or differential (interaction) effects], and block factors. An examination of an assumed model before running the experiment is often useful in determining whether the type of experiment and the design will be adequate to answer the questions of interest.

A major use of such models is to furnish a prediction of what will be observed in the experiment space if future observations are taken. After running the experiment, the coefficients included in the model are estimated on the basis of the observed results, and the assumed (theoretical) model becomes an observed (empirical) model, which contains a term representing the experimental error. The models discussed within this standard are linear with respect to the parameters to be estimated, but nonlinear relationships are included under this definition.

Example: Two factors—X_1 at two levels and X_2 at three levels—are to be studied in a 2×3 factorial experiment with replication in two blocks (a randomized block design). If it is assumed, as is frequently the case, that the response pattern can be approximated by a polynomial model, the fitted equation of the assumed model might take the form

$$Y_{est} = B_0 + B_1X_1 + B_2X_2 + B_{22}X_2{}^2 + B_{12}X_1X_2 + B_bX_b.$$

| Y_{est} (Estimated treatment response) | B_0 (constant) | B_1X_1 (linear effect of factor X_1) | B_2X_2 (linear effect of factor X_2) | $B_{22}X_2{}^2$ (curvature effect of factor X_2) | $B_{12}X_1X_2$ differential (interaction) effect of the two factors (linear) | $B_bX_b.$ (average effect of blocks) |

This notation using Y to represent the response value, X_i the predictor value, and B_i the coefficients has been commonly used in regression studies. In analysis of variance studies it has been common to use X as the response value and letters such as A and B as the factors. See also *analysis of variance.*

attributes, method of

Measurement of quality by the method of attributes consists of noting the presence (or absence) of some characteristic or attribute in each of the units in the group under consideration, and counting how many units do (or do not) possess the quality attribute, or how many such events occur in the unit, group, or area.

Note: One of the most common attribute measures for acceptance sampling is the percentage of nonconforming units. (2)

average outgoing quality (AOQ)

The expected quality of outgoing product following the use of an acceptance sampling plan for a given value of incoming product quality. (2)

Note: The AOQ is usually expressed in terms of the percentage or proportion of variant units in a series of lots or product stream and is of practical value for continuous sampling plans and lot-by-lot plans only if inspection lots that have not been accepted are sorted and variant units removed or replaced, and these lots are then included with the accepted lots. The computational formula for the AOQ depends on whether or not the sample items and the lots not accepted are discarded, and whether or not variant units detected during sampling or 100 percent inspection are replaced by acceptable units. If the incoming quality is poor (has a high level of variant units) so that a particular sampling plan may call for acceptance of only a small percentage of lots, the outgoing quality will be the same as the incoming (poor) unless the not-accepted lots are sorted and variant units removed or replaced, and these lots are then included with the accepted lots.

average outgoing quality limit (AOQL)

For a given acceptance sampling plan, the maximum AOQ over all possible levels of incoming quality. (2)

Notes:

1. For incoming lots or runs of product containing a low percentage or proportion of variant units, the AOQ consequently will be low. For incoming lots containing a high percentage or proportion of variant units, the AOQ will also be low if the variant units in the not-accepted lots have been replaced by acceptable ones, as a relatively large number of lots will be sorted and all variant units replaced, which will appreciably reduce the outgoing level of variant units. For continuous sampling, if the proportion of variant units is high, the AOQ also will be low as it will be more likely to result in 100 percent inspection, resulting in the removal (and sometimes replacement) of variant units.

The AOQL will be found at an intermediate percentage or proportion of variant units where, in lot-by-lot inspection, relatively few lots will be sorted to replace the variant units or, in continuous sampling, there will be relatively few periods of 100 percent inspection. If only the accepted lots are included in the outgoing product, the maximum AOQ will correspond to the poorest incoming quality submitted, and the concept of AOQL will not have practical value.

2. The AOQL is the maximum average outgoing quality; but, because an average is involved, the proportion of variant units in individual lots or segment of production can exceed the AOQL value.

3. In most acceptance sampling situations, the word *variant* should be replaced by *nonconforming*.

average run length (ARL)

1: (sample sense) The average number of times that a process will have been sampled and evaluated before a shift in process level is signaled.

2: (unit sense) The average number of units that will have been produced before a shift in level is signaled. (1)

Note:

A long ARL is desirable for a process located at its specified level (so as to minimize calling for unneeded investigation or corrective action), and a short ARL is desirable for a process shifted to some undesirable level (so that corrective action will be called for promptly). ARL curves are used to describe the relative quickness in detecting level shifts of various control chart systems.

average sample number (ASN)

The average number of sample units per lot used for making decisions (acceptance or nonacceptance). (2)

average total inspection (ATI)   The average number of units inspected per lot based on the sample size for accepted lots and all inspected unit in not-accepted lots. (2)

Note: This is sometimes called *average total inspected.*

B

1: The maximum probability, or risk, of making a type II error.

2: The probability or risk of failing to discover that a shift in process level of D has occurred. (1)

balanced incomplete block (BIB) design

An incomplete block design in which each block contains the same number k of different versions from the t versions of the principal factor arranged so that every pair of versions occurs together in the same number λ of blocks from the b blocks.

Example:

$t = 7 \qquad k = 4 \qquad b = 7 \qquad \lambda = 2$

The following table displays a version of the principal factor.

		1	1	2	3	6
Block		2	2	3	4	7
		3	3	4	5	1
		4	4	5	6	2
		5	5	6	7	3
		6	6	7	1	4
		7	7	1	2	5

Note: The design implies that every version of the principal factor appears the same number of times r in the experiment and that the following relations hold

$$bk = tr \text{ and } r(k-1) = \lambda(t-1)$$

For randomization, arrange the blocks and versions within each block independently at random. Because each letter in the equations just given represents an integer, it is clear that only a restricted set of combinations (t, k, b, r, λ) is possible for constructing balanced incomplete block designs.

batch   A definite quantity of some product or material produced under conditions that are considered uniform.

Note: A batch is usually smaller than a lot or population.

bias   A systematic error that contributes to the difference between a population mean of measurements or test results and an accepted reference value.

Note: Bias is a systematic error, in contrast to random error. There may be one or more bias elements contributing to the systematic error. In general, a good estimate of bias requires averaging a large number of test results representative of the population involved.

blemish   An imperfection that occurs with a severity sufficient to cause awareness, but that should not cause any real impairment with respect to intended normal, or reasonably foreseeable, usage requirements. (1)

Note: The word *blemish* is appropriate for use when a quality characteristic of a product or service is evaluated in terms of customer awareness (as opposed to conformance to specifications). There may be synonyms for *blemish* more appropriate to particular products or services.

blemished unit   A unit of product or service containing at least one blemish. (1)

Note: See note under *blemish*.

block   A subdivision of the experiment space into a group of relatively homogeneous experimental units between which the experimental error can be expected, should a similar number of units be randomly located within the entire experiment space. (5)

Note: Blocks usually are selected to allow for assignable causes, in addition to those introduced as factors to be studied (principal factors). It may be difficult, or even impossible, to keep them constant for all of the experimental units in the complete experiment. These assignable causes may be avoidable within blocks, thus providing a more homogeneous experiment subspace. The analysis of the experiment results must account for the effect of blocking the experiment. Blocks that accommodate a complete set of treatment combinations are called *complete blocks*. Those that accommodate only a portion of the complete set are called *incomplete blocks*.

Example: The term *block* originated in agricultural experiments in which a field was subdivided into sections having common conditions, such as exposure to the wind, proximity to underground water, or depth of topsoil. In other situations, blocks are based on batches of raw material, operators, the number of units run in a day, and so on.

block factors   Those assignable causes that serve as a basis for subdividing the experiment space into blocks. (5)

Note: Generally the versions of the block factors are imposed by the available experimental conditions, but sometimes they are selected in order to broaden the interpretation of the results by including a wider range of conditions. It is usually assumed that the block factors do not interact with the principal factors. When the versions are relatively close, this is often a reasonable assumption. However, if the versions differ considerably, or there is not an a priori basis for the assumption, the assumption should be verified so that an appropriate method of analysis will be chosen for the experiment data.

C

---

c (count) The count or number of events of a given classification occurring in a sample. More than one event may occur in a unit (area of opportunity), and each such event throughout the sample is counted. (1)

C_p The capability index for a stable process, defined as

$$\frac{USL - LSL}{6\sigma_{est}} \cdot (7)$$

C_{pk} The capability index that measures capability at the specification limit that has the highest chance of a part beyond the limit. Defined as the minimum (CPL, CPU). (7)

C_{pm} The capability index that takes into account the location of the mean, defined as

$$\frac{USL - LSL}{6\sqrt{\sigma^2 + (\mu - T)^2}} \cdot (7)$$

cell A grouping within specified boundaries of the values of individual observations along the abscissa of the histogram.

cell boundaries   The endpoints of the cell that contain all values that are to be included in the cell. It is customary for the cell boundaries to have one or more significant figures (usually a 5) than the values being plotted. (6)

cell deviations (d)   For ease of computation, it is often desirable to code the data by means of subtracting a constant A from all cell midpoints. The cell midpoint X_m that is chosen equal to A, the arbitrary origin (often the cell having the greatest frequency), represents the central cell. All other cells are measured in terms of the number of cells (positive or negative) that they are distant from the central cell. For the central cell having $X_m = A$, d is 0. Cells having values higher than A have positive d values, and those having values lower than A have negative d values. (6)

cell interval (i)   The distance between the cell boundaries in terms of the units plotted. (6)

cell midpoint (X_m)   The value that is the average of the two cell boundaries. It is customary to assign the value of the cell midpoint to all the observations in the cell. (6)

central line   A line on a control chart representing the long-term average or a standard value of the statistical measure being plotted. (1)

chain sampling   Sampling inspection in which the criteria for acceptance and nonacceptance of the lot depend in part on the results of the inspection of immediately preceding lots. (2)

chance causes (random causes)   Factors, generally numerous and individually of relatively small importance, that contribute to variation, but are not feasible to detect or identify. (1)

chance variation (random variation) Variation due to chance causes. (1)

characteristic A property that helps to differentiate between items of a given sample or population.

Note: The differentiation may be either quantitative (by variables) or qualitative (by attributes). (1)

clearance number (i) As associated with a continuous sampling plan, the number of successively inspected units of product that must be found acceptable during the 100 percent inspection sequence before action to change the amount of inspection can be taken. (2)

coefficient of determination (p^2 or r^2) A measure of the part of the variance for one variable that can be explained by its linear relationship with a second variable. (6)

coefficient of multiple correlation A number between 0 and 1 that indicates the degree of the combined linear relationship of several predictor variables $X_1, X_2, \ldots, X_p$ to the response variable Y. It is the simple correlation coefficient between predicted and observed values of the response variable. (6)

coefficient of partial correlation A number between -1 and 1 that indicates the degree of relationship of the response variable Y with a single one of the several predictor variables X_i, when the linear effects of one or more of the remaining predictor variables have been held at fixed levels. It is the simple correlation between the residual values of Y and X_i, given the remaining predictors. (6)

coefficient of variation A measure of relative dispersion that is the standard deviation divided by the mean and multiplied by 100 to give a percentage value. This measure cannot be used when the data take both negative and positive values or when they have been coded in such a way that the value $X = 0$ does not coincide with the origin. (6)

completely randomized design
A design in which the treatments are assigned at random to the full set of experimental units.

Note:
No block factors are involved in a completely randomized design.

completely randomized factorial design
A factorial experiment (including all replications) run in a completely randomized design. (5)

composite design
A design developed specifically for fitting second-order response surfaces, constructed by adding further selected treatment combinations to those obtained from a 2^n factorial (or its fraction). (5)

Example:
If the coded levels of each factor are -1 and $+1$ in the 2^n factorial, the $(2n + 1)$ additional combinations for a central composite design are $(0, 0, \ldots, 0)$, $(\pm\alpha, 0, 0, \ldots, 0)$, $(0, \pm\alpha, 0, \ldots, 0)$, $\ldots$, $(0, 0, \ldots, \pm\alpha)$.

The total number of treatment combinations to be tested is $(2^n + 2n + 1)$ for a 2^n factorial.

Note:
For $n = 2, 3$, and 4, the experiment requires 9, 15, and 25 units, respectively, although additional duplicate runs of the center point are usual, as compared with 9, 27, and 81 in the 3^n factorial. The reduction in experiment size results in confounding and, thereby, sacrificing all information about curvature interactions. The value of α can be chosen to make the coefficients in the quadratic polynomials as orthogonal as possible to one another, or to minimize the bias that is

created if the true form of the response surface is not quadratic.

confidence coefficient

1: The probability that the confidence interval described by a set of confidence limits actually includes the population parameter. (6)

2: The probability that an interval about a sample statistic actually includes the population parameter.

confidence limits

The endpoints of the interval about the sample statistic that is believed, with a specified confidence coefficient, to include the population parameter. (6)

confounded factorial design

A factorial experiment in which only a fraction of the total treatment combinations are run in each block and where the selection of the treatment combinations assigned to each block is arranged so that one or more prescribed effect(s) is (are) confounded with the block effect(s), while the other effects remain clear of confounding. All factorial combinations are included in the experiment. (5)

Example:

In a 2^3 factorial with only room for four treatment combinations per block, the ABC interaction (ABC: $- (1) + a + b - ab + c - ac - bc + abc$) can be sacrificed through confounding with blocks without loss of any other effect if the blocks include the following treatment combinations.

Block 1	Block 2
(1)	a
ab	b
ac	c
bc	abc

Note: The treatment combinations to be assigned to each block can be determined once the effect (or effects) to be confounded is (are) defined. Where only one term is to be confounded with blocks, as in this example, those with a positive sign are assigned to one block and those with a negative sign to the other. There are generalized rules for more complex situations. A check on all of the other effects (*a*, *b*, *ab*, and so on) will show balance of the plus and minus signs in each block, thus eliminating any confounding with blocks for them.

confounding Combining indistinguishably the main effect of a factor, or a differential effect between factors (interactions), with the effects of other factor(s), block factor(s), or interaction(s). (5)

Note: Confounding is an important technique that permits the effective use of specified blocks in some experiment designs. This is accomplished by deliberately preselecting certain effects or differential effects as being of little interest, and arranging the design so that they are confounded with block effects, or other preselected principal factor or differential effects, while keeping the other more important effects free from such complications. Sometimes, however, confounding results from inadvertent changes to a design during the running of an experiment, or to incomplete planning of the design, and serves to diminish, or even to invalidate, the effectiveness of an experiment.

See *confounded factorial design* and *factorial experiments with partial confounding* for examples of confounding effects or differential effects (interactions) with block effects. See *fractional factorial design* and *aliases* when each effect is confounded with one or more other effects.

continuous sampling plan

A plan intended for application to a continuous flow of individual units of product that (1) involves acceptance or nonacceptance on a unit-by-unit basis and (2) uses alternate periods of 100 percent inspection and sampling depending on the quality of the observed product. (2)

Note: Continuous sampling plans are usually characterized by requiring that each period of 100 percent inspection be continued until a specified number i of consecutively inspected units are found to have no variant units. These plans may be single-level or multilevel.

contrast

A linear function of the observations for which the sum of the coefficients is zero. With observations $Y_1, Y_2, \ldots, Y_n$, the linear function $a_1 Y_1 + a_2 Y_2 + \ldots + a_n Y_n$ is a contrast if and only if $\Sigma a_i = 0$. (5)

Example: 1. A factor is applied at three levels and the results represented by A_1, A_2, and A_3. If the levels are equally spaced, the first logical question to ask might be whether there is an overall linear trend. This could be done by comparing A_1 and A_3, the extremes of A in the experiment. A second question might be whether there is evidence that the response pattern shows curvature rather than a simple linear trend. Here the average of A_1 and A_3 could be compared to A_2. (If there is no curvature, A_2 should fall on the line connecting A_1 and A_3, or, in other words, be equal to their average.)

The contrast coefficients for question 1 would be displayed like this.

$$
\begin{array}{ccc}
A_1 & A_2 & A_3 \\
-1 & 0 & +1 \\
-A_1 & & +A_3
\end{array}
$$

While those for question 2 would appear as follows.

$$-\tfrac{1}{2} \quad +1 \quad -\tfrac{1}{2}$$
$$-\tfrac{1}{2}A_1 \quad +A_2 \quad -\tfrac{1}{2}A_3$$

This example illustrates a regression-type study of equally spaced continuous variables. It is frequently more convenient to use integers rather than fractions for contrast coefficients. In such a case, the coefficients for contrast 2 would appear as $(-1, +2, -1)$.

2. Another example dealing with discrete versions of a factor might lead to a different pair of questions. Say there are three sources of supply, one of which, A_1, uses a new manufacturing technique while the other two, A_2 and A_3, use the customary technique. First, does vendor A_1 with the new technique seem to differ from A_2 and A_3 using the old technique? Contrast A_1 with the average of A_2 and A_3. Second, do the two suppliers using the customary technique differ? Contrast A_2 and A_3. The pattern of contrast coefficients is similar to that for the previous problem, though the interpretation of the results will differ.

The contrast coefficients for question 1 would be displayed like this.

$$A_1 \quad A_2 \quad A_3$$
$$-2 \quad +1 \quad +1$$
$$-2A_1 \quad +A_2 \quad +A_3$$

While those for question 2 would appear as follows.

$$0 \quad -1 \quad +1$$
$$-A_2 \quad +A_3$$

Note: The coefficients for a contrast may be selected arbitrarily provided the $\sum a_1 = 0$ condition is met. There will be an a_1 value for each response, including one for each replicate. Questions of logical interest from an experiment may be expressed as contrasts with carefully selected coefficients. See the previous examples. As indicated in the examples, the response for each treatment combination will have associated with it a set of coefficients. The number of linearly independent contrasts in an experiment is equal to one less than the number of treatments. Sometimes the term *contrast* is used only to refer to the pattern of the coefficients, but the usual interpretation is the algebraic sum of the responses multiplied by the appropriate coefficients.

contrast analysis   A technique for estimating the parameters of a model and making hypothesis tests on preselected linear combinations of the treatments (contrasts). (5)

Example: Half replicate of a 2^4 factorial experiment with factors A, B, and C (X_1, X_2, and X_3) being quantitative, and factor D (X_4) being qualitative. Defining contrast $I = +ABCD = X_1X_2X_3X_4$.

The table of contrast coefficients shown on page 31 pertains to notes 1 and 2.

Notes: 1. The center is not a contrast ($\sum X_i \neq 0$), but it is convenient in the contrast analysis calculations to treat it as one.
2. Once the contrast coefficients of the main effects (X_1, X_2, X_3, and X_4) are filled in the table, the coefficients for all interaction and other second, or higher-order effects can be derived as products ($X_{ij} = X_iX_j$) of the appropriate terms.

Table of contrast coefficients

Source						Treatments					
		(1)	ab	ac	bc	ad	bd	cd	abcd		
Center	X_0	+1	+1	+1	+1	+1	+1	+1	+1	Note 1
A (+BCD): pH (8.0, 9.0)	X_1	-1	+1	+1	-1	+1	-1	-1	+1	
B (+ACD): SO_4 (10cc, 16cc)	X_2	-1	+1	-1	+1	-1	+1	-1	+1	
C (+ABD): Temp (120°, 150°)	X_3	-1	-1	+1	+1	-1	-1	+1	+1	
D (+ABC): Factory (PQ)	X_4	-1	-1	-1	-1	+1	+1	+1	+1	
$AB + CD$ $X_1X_2 = X_{12}$		+1	+1	-1	-1	-1	-1	+1	+1	
$AC + BD$ $X_1X_3 = X_{13}$		+1	-1	+1	-1	-1	+1	-1	+1	Note 2
$AD + BC$ $X_1X_4 = X_{14}$		+1	-1	-1	+1	+1	-1	-1	+1	

Contrast analysis table

Source	Contrast $\sum_i X_{ij} Y_i$	Divisor $\sum_i X_{ij}^2$	Student's t ratio $(\sum_i X_{ij} Y_i)/s\sqrt{\sum_i X_{ij}^2}$	Regression coefficient $B_j = (\sum_i X_{ij} Y_i)/\sum_i X_{ij}^2$
X_0: Center	$\sum X_0 Y$	$\sum X_0^2$	$(\sum X_0 Y)/s\sqrt{\sum X_0^2}$	$B_0 = (\sum Y_0 Y)/\sum X_0^2$
X_1: $A + BCD$	$\sum X_1 Y$	$\sum X_1^2$	$(\sum X_1 Y)/s\sqrt{\sum X_1^2}$	$B_1 = (\sum X_1 Y)/\sum X_1^2$
X_2: $B + ACD$	$\sum X_2 Y$	$\sum X_2^2$	$(\sum X_2 Y)/s\sqrt{\sum X_2^2}$	$B_2 = (\sum X_2 Y)/\sum X_2^2$
X_3: $C + ABD$	$\sum X_3 Y$	$\sum X_3^2$	$(\sum X_3 Y)/s\sqrt{\sum X_3^2}$	$B_3 = (\sum X_3 Y)/\sum X_3^2$
X_4: $D + ABC$	$\sum X_4 Y$	$\sum X_4^2$	$(\sum X_4 Y)/s\sqrt{\sum X_4^2}$	$B_4 = (\sum X_4 Y)/\sum X_4^2$
X_{12}: $AB + CD$	$\sum X_{12} Y$	$\sum X_{12}^2$	$(\sum X_{12} Y)/s\sqrt{\sum X_{12}^2}$	$B_{12} = (\sum X_{12} Y)/\sum X_{12}^2$
X_{13}: $AC + BD$	$\sum X_{13} Y$	$\sum X_{13}^2$	$(\sum X_{13} Y)/s\sqrt{\sum X_{13}^2}$	$B_{13} = (\sum X_{13} Y)/\sum X_{13}^2$
X_{14}: $AD + BD$	$\sum X_{14} Y$	$\sum X_{14}^2$	$(\sum X_{14} Y)/s\sqrt{\sum X_{14}^2}$	$B_{14} = (\sum X_{14} Y)/\sum X_{14}^2$

The notation for contrast analysis usually uses Y to indicate the response variable and X to indicate the predictor variables.

3. The measure of experimental error, s, can be obtained in various ways. If the experiment is replicated, s is the square root of the pooled variances of the pairs for each treatment combination. (Each row of X values would be expanded to account for the additional observations in the contrast analysis computations.) If some effects were felt to be pseudoreplicates (say no interactions were logical), multiplying the contrast by the regression coefficient of these terms forms a sum of squares (as in analysis of variance), and these would be summed and divided by the number of terms involved to give s^2. Also in many experiments, past experience may already provide an estimate of this error.

An assumed model could be given as

$$Y = \beta_0 + \beta_1 X_{1i} + \beta_2 X_{2i} + \beta_3 X_{3i} + \beta_4 X_{4i} + e$$

In a simple two-level experiment such as this, the regression coefficient measures the half effect of shifting a factor, say pH, between its low and high level, or the effect of shifting from a center level to the high level. In general, substitution of the appropriate contrast coefficients for the X terms in the model will permit any desired comparisons. The difference between quantitative and qualitative factors lies in the interpretation. Because a unit of X_1 represents a pH shift of 0.5, there is a meaningful translation into physical units. On the other hand, the units of the qualitative variable (factories) have no significance other than for identification and in the substitution process to obtain estimates of the average response value.

4. Contrast analysis involves a systematic tabulation and analysis format usable for both simple and complex designs. When any set of orthogonal contrasts is used, the procedure, as in the example, is straightforward. When terms are not orthogonal, the orthogonalization process is also systematic and can be programmed.

control chart   A graphical method for evaluating whether a process is or is not in a state of statistical control. (The determinations are made through comparison of the values of some statistical measure(s) for an ordered series of samples, or subgroups, with control limits.) (1)

Note: A control chart is used to make decisions about a process. There are a variety of specific charts, each designed for the type of decisions to be made, the nature of the data, and the type of statistical measure used. The term *control chart* was for many years synonymous with *Shewhart control chart*, being based on the original work by Shewhart [W. A. Shewhart, *Economic Control of Quality of Manufactured Product* (New York: C. Van Nostrand Company, 1931)]. There are now several other distinct types or major variations in use.

The emphasis of the control chart, as contrasted to the acceptance control chart, is on the process being in control rather than a direct evaluation of whether the measure of the product or service satisfies tolerance requirements. The control chart, however, is sometimes used in an acceptance sense, calling for action or investigation when a process is deemed to have shifted from its standard level.

control chart (no standard given)   A control chart whose control limits are based on the sample or subgroup data plotted on the chart.

Note: This type of control chart is used to determine whether observed values of $\overline{X}$, R, p, and so on for a series of samples vary among themselves by an amount greater than should be attributed to chance. Control charts based entirely on the data from the samples being evaluated are used for detecting lack of constancy of the cause system. This type of chart is particularly useful in research and development stages to determine whether a new process or product is reproducible and whether test methods are repeatable.

control chart (standard given) A control chart whose control limits are based on adopted standard values applicable to the statistical measures plotted on the chart.

Note: This type of control chart is used to discover whether observed values of $\overline{X}$, c, p, and so on for samples differ from standard values $\overline{X}_0$, c_0, p_0, and so on by an amount greater than should be attributed to chance. The standard value may be based on representative prior data, or an economic value based on consideration of needs of service and cost of production, or a desired or aimed-at value designated by a specification. The standard value of the standard deviation should almost invariably be based on representative prior data. It is assumed that the process is capable of being, and intended to be, operated at the designated standard values. Any prior data being used to set limits should be checked to assure that they are in control.

The use of the subscript zero (for example, $\overline{X}_0$, c_0, p_0) to designate standard levels is recommended to avoid confusion with exponents. There has been a long tradition of using the prime notation ($\overline{X}'$, c', p') for this purpose, and this will continue to be an accepted alternative along with a combination of both ($\overline{X}'_0$, c'_0, p'_0). Generally, the use of a prime notation is an indication that the standard value is to be treated as if it were the population value, although Greek letters are sometimes used to indicate this.

control chart factor
A factor, usually varying with sample size, to convert specified statistics or parameters into a central line value or control limit appropriate to the control chart. (1)

control chart method
The method of using control charts to determine whether or not processes are in a stable state. (1)

control limits
Limits on a control chart that are used as criteria for signaling the need for action, or for judging whether a set of data does or does not indicate a state of statistical control. (1)

Note:
When warning limits are used, the control limits are often called *action limits.* Action may be in the form of investigation of the source(s) of an assignable cause, making a process adjustment, or terminating a process. Criteria other than control limits are also used frequently.

Control limit formulas for Shewhart attribute control charts and control limit formulas for Shewhart control charts are given in the following tables.

Control limit formulas for Shewhart attribute control charts

| Statistic | No standard given | |
	Central line	3σ control limit
p	$\bar{p}$	$\bar{p} \pm 3\sqrt{\bar{p}(1-\bar{p})/n}$
np	$\overline{np}$	$\overline{np} \pm 3\sqrt{\overline{np}(1-\bar{p})}$
c	$\bar{c}$	$\bar{c} \pm 3\sqrt{\bar{c}}$
u	$\bar{u}$	$\bar{u} \pm 3\sqrt{\bar{u}/n}$
c/n	$\bar{c}/n$	$(\bar{c}/n) \pm (3/n)\sqrt{\bar{c}}$
$Q = \Sigma w_i c_i$	$\Sigma w_i \bar{c}_i$	$\Sigma w_i \bar{c}_i \pm \sqrt{\Sigma(w_i^2 \bar{c}_i)}$
$Q/n = \Sigma w_i c_i/n$	$\Sigma w_i \bar{c}_i/n$	$\Sigma w_i \bar{c}_i/n \pm (3/n)\sqrt{\Sigma(w_i^2 \bar{c}_i)}$
$D = \Sigma d_i c_i$	$\Sigma d_i \bar{c}_i$	$\Sigma d_i \bar{c}_i \pm 3\sqrt{\Sigma(d_i^2 \bar{c}_i)}$

Statistic	Standard given	
	Central line	3σ control limit
p	p_0	$p_0 \pm 3\sqrt{p_0(1-p_0)/n}$
np	np_0	$np_0 \pm 3\sqrt{np_0(1-p_0)}$
c	c_0	$c_0 \pm 3\sqrt{c_0}$
u	u_0	$u_0 \pm 3\sqrt{u_0/n}$
c/n	c_0/n	$(c_0/n) \pm (3/n)\sqrt{c_0}$
$Q = \Sigma w_i c_i$	$\Sigma w_i c_{0i}$	$\Sigma w_i c_{0i} \pm 3\sqrt{\Sigma(w_i^2 c_{0i})}$
$Q/n = \Sigma w_i c_i/n$	$\Sigma w_i c_{0i}/n$	$\Sigma w_i c_{0i}/n \pm (3/n)\sqrt{\Sigma(w_i^2 c_{0i})}$
$D = \Sigma d_i c_i$	$\Sigma d_i c_{0i}$	$\Sigma d_i c_{0i} \pm 3\sqrt{\Sigma(d_i'^2 c_{0i})}$

Notes: 1. To avoid confusion with exponents, the use of the subscript zero (as in c_0, p_0, and u_0) to designate standard levels is recommended. However, there has been a long tradition of using the prime notation (for example, c', p', and u') for this purpose, and this will continue to be an accepted alternative along with a combination of both (for example, c'_0, p'_0, u'_0).

2. The control limits for these charts are ±3 standard deviations (standard errors) computed on the assumption that the process was in control during the base period.

3. For the p chart only, if p is expressed as a percent instead of the more customary proportion or fraction, it is necessary to replace the 1 in the control limit formulas with 100.

4. If Q/n is used rather than Q,

$$s_{Q/n} = \frac{1}{n}\sqrt{\Sigma_i^2 c_i}.$$

Control limit formulas for Shewhart variables control charts and control limit formulas for Shewhart control charts are shown in the following table.

Control limit formulas for Shewhart variables control charts

Statistic	Central line	3σ control limits
	No standard given	
$\overline{X}$	$\overline{\overline{X}}$	$\overline{\overline{X}} \pm A_2\overline{R}$, $\overline{\overline{X}} \pm A_3\overline{s}$
X	$\overline{X}$	$\overline{X} \pm E_2R$, $\overline{X} \pm E_3\overline{s}$
R	$\overline{R}$	$D_3\overline{R}$, $D_4\overline{R}$
s	$\overline{s}$	$B_3\overline{s}$, $B_4\overline{s}$

Statistic	Central line	3σ control limits
	Standard given	
$\overline{X}$	$\overline{X}_0$ or μ	$\overline{X}_0 \pm A\sigma_0$
X	X_0 or μ	$X_0 \pm 3\sigma_0$
R	R_0 or $d_2\sigma_0$	$D_1\sigma_0$, $D_2\sigma_0$
x	s_0 or $c_4\sigma_0$	$B_5\sigma_0$, $B_6\sigma_0$

Note: Where the population standard deviation σ is known, σ may be used rather than σ_0 in the formulas for "Standard given." To avoid confusion with exponents, the use of the subscript zero to designate standard levels is recommended ($\overline{X}_0$, σ_0). However, there has been a long tradition of using the prime notation ($\overline{X}'$, σ') for this purpose, and this will continue to be an accepted alternative along with a combination of both ($\overline{X}'_0$, σ'_0).

Y is often used instead of X to represent an observation. In such cases, Y, $\overline{Y}$, $\overline{\overline{Y}}$, Y_0, and $\overline{Y}_0$ should be substituted where appropriate in the formulas just given. (1)

correlation and regression

1. Population slope of regression line β_1:

$$b_1 - t_{(n-2,\ \alpha/2)}s_{b_1} \qquad b_1 + t_{(n-2,\alpha/2)}s_{b_1}$$

2. Population intercept of regression line β_0:

$$b_0 - t_{(n-2,\ \alpha/2)}s_{b_0} \qquad b_0 + t_{(n-2,\alpha/2)}s_{b_0}$$

3. Population regression line $Y_{est} = \beta_0 + \beta_1 X$:

$$(b_0 + b_1 X) - t_{(n-2,\alpha/2)} S_{\hat{Y}}$$
$$(b_0 + b_1 X) + t_{(n-2,\alpha/2)} 5_{\hat{y}}$$

4. Population correlation coefficient p is shown in the nomograph in Figure 2.

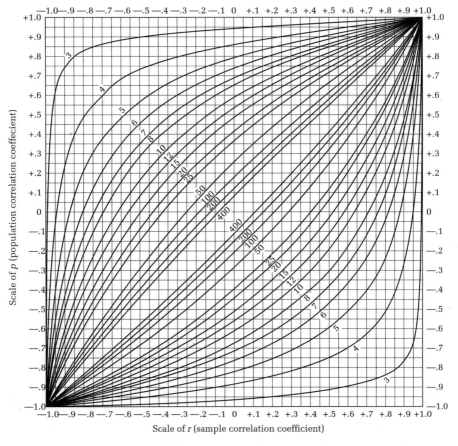

Figure 2. 95% confidence limits for correlation coefficients. Sample size given by numbers on curves. Reproduced with permission.

Correlation coefficient (simple correlation coefficient) (p_{xy} or p for populations, r_{xy} or r for samples)

A number between -1 and 1 that indicates the degree of linear relationship between two sets of numbers:

$$r_{xy} = \frac{s_{xy}}{s_x s_y} = \frac{n\Sigma XY - \Sigma Y}{\sqrt{[n\Sigma X^2 - (\Sigma X)^2 - (\Sigma Y)^2]}}.$$

Correlations of -1 and $+1$ represent perfect linear agreement between two variables; $r = 0$ implies no linear relationship at all. (6)

Covariance (σ_{xy} for populations, s_{xy} for samples)

A measure of the relationship between pairs of observations from two variables. (6)

Covariance matrix (Σ for populations, s for samples)

A symmetric matrix whose diagonals are the variances and whose $i \neq j$ elements are the covariances of the variables corresponding to the i and j columns. (6)

$$s_{xy} = \frac{\Sigma(X_i - \overline{X})(Y_i - \overline{Y})}{n - 1} = \frac{n\Sigma XY - (\Sigma)}{n(n - 1)}.$$

CPL

The lower capability index defined as

$$\frac{(\overline{X} - LSL)}{3\sigma_{est}}. \text{ (7)}$$

CPU

The upper capability index, defined as

$$\frac{USL - \overline{X}}{3\sigma_{est}}. \text{ (7)}$$

CR   The capability ratio for a stable process, defined as

$$\frac{6\sigma_{est}}{(USL - LSL)} \, . \, (8)$$

Cumulative frequency distribution   A set of the various values that individual observations may have and the frequency of the occurrence of observations having a value less than or greater than the particular cell boundary. (6)

Cumulative sum chart; cusum chart   A control chart on which the plotted value is the cumulative sum of deviations of successive sample statistics from a target value. The ordinate of each plotted point represents the algebraic sum of the previous ordinate and the most recent deviation from the target.

Note: Cusum charts are generally interpreted by masks superimposed on the chart, a signal occurring if the path of the cusum intersects or touches the boundary of the mask.

D

D	The smallest shift in process level that it is desired to detect, stated in terms of original units.
D (demerit)	A weighting assigned to a classification of an event or events to provide a means of obtaining a weighted quality score. (1)
Note:	See also *Q (quality score)*.
δ	The smallest shift in process level that it is desired to detect, stated in terms of the number of standard errors of the average.

$$\delta = D/\sigma_{\bar{x}}$$

defect	A departure of a quality characteristic from its intended level or state that occurs with a severity sufficient to cause an associated product or service not to satisfy intended normal, or reasonably foreseeable, usage requirements. (1)

Defects will generally be classified by their degree of seriousness:

Class 1	Very serious	Leads directly to severe injury or catastrophic economic loss
Class 2	Serious	Leads directly to significant injury or significant economic loss

| Class 3 | Major | Related to major problems with respect to intended normal, or reasonably foreseeable, use |
| Class 4 | Minor | Related to minor problems with respect to intended normal, or reasonably foreseeable, use |

The word *critical* is sometimes used for the first two classes instead of *very serious* and *serious*. It is best to avoid the use of this word whenever possible because of its many other uses. For example, critical list in a hospital (implying threat of death); critical dimension (product will not work unless this dimension meets specifications); critical look (referring to more careful examination).

Rating systems to evaluate the performance of a product or service may require a second modifier to describe the likelihood that the potential defect will be found in the operation of the product or service. Modifiers for likelihood of occurrence include

- Virtually certain
- Substantially above a 50 percent chance
- Somewhat above a 50 percent chance
- Around a 50 percent chance
- Somewhat below a 50 percent chance
- Substantially under a 50 percent chance
- Virtually no chance

Note: The word *defect* is appropriate for use when a quality characteristic of a product or service is evaluated in terms of usage (as contrasted to conformance to specifications).

defective (defective unit)

A unit of product or service containing at least one defect, or having several imperfections that in combination cause the unit not to satisfy intended normal, or reasonably foreseeable, usage requirements. (1)

Note:

The word *defective* is appropriate for use when a unit of product or service is evaluated in terms of usage (as contrasted to conformance to specifications).

degrees of freedom

A parameter that, in general, is the number of independent comparisons available to estimate a specific parameter and that serves as a means of entering certain statistical tables. (6)

designated imperfections (delta)

A category of imperfections that, because of their type and/or magnitude or severity, are to be treated as an event for control purposes. (1)

Note:

The discussion in the comments under *imperfection* emphasizes the use of information about imperfections for control purposes. Some imperfections will be so small, or of such a nature that they are not worth the cost and effort of recording or, if recorded, of being routinely analyzed. Those that are designated to be appropriate for the specific analysis involved are termed *designated imperfections*. Because of the length of this expression, a symbol Δ is sometimes used and the term referred to as *delta*.

Designated imperfections is a general term that includes several categories and classifications that will usually be identified more specifically. The categories may include a single imperfection type or families, which may range from related imperfection types (some cause system or appearance) to broad groupings (possibly even all types). Classifications are groupings within a category of severity or magnitude intervals (for example, single classifications: all scratches over 1 mm in length; parts failing to go or not go through a go–no go gage; and so on; multiple classifications: scratches between 1 mm and 2 mm, between 2 and 3 mm, and so on; or falling on a judgment scale above the upper limit of guide B but below the upper limit of guide D, above the upper limit of guide D but below the upper limit of guide F, and so on). The classifications include grouping in cells or classes of variables data to form attribute measures. The event plotted as a designated imperfection may be a category or a classification, rather than the full range of an imperfection.

design of experiments (experiment design)   The arrangement in which an experimental program is to be conducted, and the selection of the versions (levels) of one or more factors or factor combinations to be included in the experiment. (5)

Note: The purpose of designing an experiment is to provide the most efficient and economical methods of reaching valid and relevant conclusions from the experiment. The selection of an appropriate design for any experiment is a function of many considerations, such as the type of questions to be answered, the degree of generality to be attached to the conclusions, the magnitude of the effect for which a high probability of detection (power) is desired, the homogeneity of the experimental units, and the cost of performing the experiment. A properly designed experiment will permit relatively simple statistical interpretation of the results, which may not be possible otherwise. The arrangement includes the randomization procedure for allocating treatments to experimental units. The term *experimental design* is also frequently used.

See also *experimental unit, factor, treatment.*

deviation (measurement sense)

The difference between a measurement or quasi measurement and its stated value or intended level. (1)

Note:

A deviation, as used in a measurement sense, should be stated as a difference in terms of the appropriate data units. Sometimes these units will be original measurement units; sometimes they will be quasi measurements (that is, a scaling rating of subjective judgments); sometimes they will be designated values representing all continuous or discrete measurements falling in defined cells or classes.

double sampling

Sampling inspection in which the inspection of the first sample of size n_1 leads to a decision to accept a lot; not to accept it; or to take a second sample of size n_2, and the inspection of the second sample then leads to a decision to accept or not to accept the lot. (2)

duplication

The execution of a treatment more than once under similar conditions. (5)

Note:

Duplication, as contrasted to replication, refers to a single element of an experiment. Duplication usually involves a fresh experimental unit, such as another sample or, when a single unit is involved, an independent resetting of the levels of the factors being studied on that unit. When duplicate observations are made on the same sample or unchanged settings, these should be identified as *duplicate observations* rather than as *duplicates*, to reflect the narrower degree of duplication.

E

---

element See *unit*. (1)

event An occurrence of some attribute. (1)

Note: Attribute data deal with the occurrence of events. Individual types of events might be further classified by modifiers of size, quantity, location, degree of seriousness, likelihood of occurrence, or other useful subdivision.

evolutionary operation (EVOP) A sequential form of experimentation conducted in production facilities during regular production. (5)

Note: The principal theses of EVOP are that knowledge to improve the process should be obtained along with a product, and that designed experiments using relatively small shifts in factor levels (within production tolerances) can yield this knowledge at minimum cost. The range of variation of the factors for any one EVOP experiment is usually quite small, in order to avoid making out-of-tolerance product, and this may require considerable replication so as to reduce the effect of random variation.

experimental error The variation in the responses (test results) caused by extraneous variables, other than those due to factors and blocks, that adds a degree of uncertainty to the observed response value. (5)

Note: It is a common characteristic of experiments that, when they are repeated, their results vary from trial to trial, even though the experimental materials, environmental conditions, and experimental operations are carefully controlled. Therefore, the occurrence of experimental error is inevitable in practical experimentation. This variation introduces a degree of uncertainty into conclusions that are drawn from the results, and therefore must be taken into account in reaching conclusions. See also *residual error.* Experimental error is usually measured in an experiment as a pooled variance of sets of duplicate observations.

experimental unit A portion of the experiment space to which a treatment is applied or assigned in the experiment. (5)

Example: The unit may be a patient in a hospital, a group of animals, a production batch, a section of a compartmented tray, and so on.

experiment space The materials, equipment, environmental conditions, and so forth that are available for conducting an experiment. (5)

Note: That portion of the experiment space restricted to the range of versions (levels) of the factors to be studied in the experiment is sometimes called the *factor space.* Some elements of the experiment space may be identified with blocks and be considered block factors.

F

factor   An assignable cause that may affect the responses (test results) and of which different versions (levels) are included in the experiment. (5)

Note: Factors may be quantitative, such as temperature, speed of execution, and voltage applied, or they may be qualitative, such as the variety of a material, presence or absence of a catalyst, and the type of equipment. Those factors that are to be studied in the experiment are sometimes called *principal factors.*
See also *block factors, experiment space.*

factorial
experiment
(general)   An experiment in which all possible treatment combinations formed from two or more factors, each being studied at two or more versions (levels), are examined so that interactions (differential effects) as well as main effects can be estimated. (5)

Note: The term is descriptive of the combining of the various factors in all possible combinations, but in itself does not describe the experiment design in which these combinations, or subset of these combinations, will be studied. The most commonly used designs for the selected arrangement of the factorial treatment combinations are the completely randomized design, the randomized block design, and the balanced incomplete block design, but others also are used.

A factorial experiment is usually described symbolically as the product of the number of versions (levels) of each factor. For example, an experiment based on three levels of factor A, two versions of factor B, and four levels of factor C would be referred to as a $3 \times 2 \times 4$ factorial. The product of these numbers indicates the number of factorial treatments. When a factorial experiment includes factors all having the same number of versions (levels), the description is usually given in terms of the number of levels raised to the power equal to the number of factors, n. Thus, three factors all run at two levels would be referred to as a 2^3 factorial (n being equal to 3) and would have 8 factorial treatment combinations.

Some commonly used notations for describing the treatment combinations for a factorial experiment include the following.

1. Use a letter to indicate the factor and a numerical subscript to represent the version (level) of the factor. For example, for three factors A, B, and C in a $2 \times 3 \times 2$ factorial, the 12 combinations would be $A_1B_1C_1$, $A_2B_1C_1$, $A_1B_2C_1$, $A_2B_2C_1$, $A_1B_3C_1$, $A_2B_3C_1$, $A_1B_1C_2$, $A_2B_1C_2$, $A_1B_2C_2$, $A_2B_2C_2$, $A_1B_3C_2$, $A_2B_3C_2$. Sometimes only the subscripts, listed in the same order as the factors, are used: 111, 211, 121, 221, 131, 231, 112, 212, 122, 222, 132, 232. A variation that permits the use of modulo 2 and modulo 3 arithmetic for the purpose of listing the treatment combinations in blocked and fractional designs is 000, 100, 010, 110, 020, 120, 001, 101, 011, 111, 021, 121.
2. Describe the levels in terms of the number of unit deviations from the center level, in-

cluding sign. (In the case of an even number of levels where there is no actual treatment at the center level, the coefficients describing the levels are usually given in terms of half-unit deviations. For example, in a two-level experiment, if a unit of length between levels is 4 mm, the -1 coefficient might be assigned to 3 mm and the $+1$ to 7 mm with 0 being assigned to the nonincluded 5 mm level.) In the previous example, the code would appear as $(-1, -1, -1)$; $(+1, -1, -1)$; $(-1, 0, -1)$; $(+1, 0, -1)$; $(-1, +1, -1)$; $(+1, +1, -1)$; $(-1, -1, +1)$; $(+1, -1, +1)$; $(-1, 0, +1)$; $(+1, 0, +1)$; $(-1, +1, +1)$; $(+1, +1, +1)$. This descriptive coding has many advantages, particularly in analyzing contrasts when levels are equally spaced. Unequal spacing of the levels or weighted emphasis for the various versions can also be reflected in the coefficients.

factorial experiments with partial confounding

A factorial experiment with several replicates in which some main effects or interactions confounded in other replicates are free from confounding. (5)

Example:

In a 2^3 factorial experiment requiring the use of blocks of four, and carried out with two replicates, the following arrangement is selected so that the *ABC* interaction is confounded in rep-

Replicate 1		Replicate 2	
Block 1	Block 2	Block 1	Block 2
(1)	*a*	(1)	*b*
ab	*b*	*a*	*c*
ac	*c*	*bc*	*ab*
bc	*abc*	*abc*	*ac*

licate 1 and the *BC* interaction is confounded in replicate 2.

The estimate of *BC* can be obtained only from replicate 1 and that of *ABC* only from replicate 2. The remaining estimates of *A*, *B*, *C*, *AB*, and *AC* are obtainable using both replicates, and therefore will have greater precision.

failure

The termination, due to one or more defects, of the ability of an item, product, or service to perform its required function when called upon to do so. (6)

failure mechanism

The physical, chemical, or mechanical process that caused the defect and failure. (6)

failure mode

The type of defect contributing to a failure.

Note:

Examples are an open- or short-circuit condition, a gain change, leakage, fracture, and so on. (6)

fractional factorial design

A factorial experiment in which only an adequately chosen fraction of the treatment combinations required for the complete factorial experiment is selected to be run. This procedure is sometimes called *fractional replication*. (5)

Note:

The fraction selected is obtained by choosing one or several defining contrasts, which are considered of minor importance, or negligible, generally interaction(s) of high order. These defining contrasts cannot be estimated and, thus, are sacrificed. "Adequately chosen" refers to selection according to specified rules that include consideration of effects to be confounded and aliased (see also *aliases* and *confounding*).

Fractional factorial designs are often used very effectively in screening tests to determine which factor or factors are effective, or as part of a sequential series of tests; but there are risks of getting biased estimates of main effects or of misjudging the relative importance of various factors. When there are a large number of treatment combinations resulting from a large number of factors to be tested, it is often impractical to test all the combinations with one experiment. In such cases resort may be made to a fractional, that is a partial, replication. The usefulness of these designs stems from the fact that, in general, higher-order interactions are not likely to occur. When this assumption is not valid, biased estimates will result.

Example: Two half-replicates of a 2^4 factorial.
Defining contrast: *ABCD*

+	−
abcd	*abc*
ab	*abd*
ac	*acd*
ad	*bcd*
bc	*a*
bd	*b*
cd	*c*
(1)	*d*

Either of these half-replicates can be used as a fractional replicate.

Note: In the example, the factorial combinations in the first column are those with a + sign when the *ABCD* defining contrast is expanded, and those in the second column are those with a minus sign. $ABCD = (a − 1)(b − 1)(c − 1)(d − 1)$. Because only those elements of the *ABCD* interaction having the same sign are run, no *ABCD* contrast measure is obtainable, so that the *ABCD* interaction is completely confounded and unestimable. In addition, it will be found that because only half of the full factorial experiment is run, each contrast represents two effects.

From the + sign fractional replicate in the previous example, we would compute the factorial effects as follows:

$$A = (abcd) + (ab) + (ac) + (ad) - (bc) - (bd)$$
$$- (cd) - (1) = BCD;$$

$$AB = (abcd) + (ab) + (cd) + (1) - (ac) - (ad)$$
$$- (bc) - (bd) = CD.$$

Effects represented by the same contrast are named *aliases* (see *aliases*). Note that, had the complete set of factorial treatments been run instead of only half of them, the A and BCD or AB and BC effects would no longer be identical. That is, $A = (a - 1)(b + 1)(c + 1)(d + 1)$ is not equal to $BCD = (a + 1)(b - 1)(c - 1)(d - 1)$ when all 16 combinations are included instead of only eight. This example, and the comments thereon, have been limited to the 2^n factorial experiments. A comparable, but more difficult, approach is available for factorials involving more than two versions, but another approach to these situations is through the use of the composite design.

frequency distribution A set of all the various values that individual observations may have and the frequency of their occurrence in the sample or population.

fully nested experiment A nested experiment in which the second factor is nested within levels (versions) of the first factor and each succeeding factor is nested within versions of the previous factor. (5)

Example:

Factor A version		A_1				A_2	
Factor B version	/		\		/		\
	B_1		B_2		B_3		B_4
Factor C version	/ \		/ \		/ \		/ \
	C_1 C_2		C_3 C_4		C_5 C_6		C_7 C_8

G

---

grade
A category or rank indicator of the totality of features and characteristics of a product or service intended for the same functional use or purpose, oriented at a specified cost-related consumer/user market.

Note:
Grade reflects that additional features and characteristics may be desirable, usually for added cost, and that a different version of the product or service is thus defined. (6)

Graeco-Latin square
A design involving four factors in which the combination of the versions of any one of them with the versions of the other three appears once and only once. (5)

An example of a Graeco-Latin square follows.

		Factor 2 (columns)		
		1	2	3
	1	$A\alpha$	$B\gamma$	$C\beta$
Factor 1 (rows)	2	$B\beta$	$C\alpha$	$A\gamma$
	3	$C\gamma$	$A\beta$	$B\alpha$

Factor 4 (Greek letters)

Frequently, numerical subscripts are used in place of Greek letters. Versions of the third factor are shown by the Latin letters.

Note: The comments in the note under *Latin square* are pertinent here also, modified by the extension to four factors. A Graeco-Latin square does not exist for squares of size 6.

A generalization of the Graeco-Latin square for more than three block factors is known as the *hyper Graeco-Latin square.*

grouped   A frequency distribution based on the grouping
frequency   into a cell of several adjacent values that indi-
distribution   vidual observations may take. (6)

H

histogram   A plot of frequency distribution in the form of rectangles whose bases are equal to the cell interval and whose areas are proportional to the frequencies. (6)

I

imperfection   A departure of a quality characteristic from its intended level or state without any association with conformance to specification requirements or to the usability of a product or service. (Usually imperfections will be rated on a severity scale or measured as deviations and, unless of high severity or magnitude, would be reasonably expected in a product or service of acceptable quality. (1)

Notes: 1. An alternate term for *imperfection* is *quality characteristic departure*.

2. For quality characteristics where there is no designated intended level so that a departure is not definable, *observed measurements* will serve the same role as *imperfection* in providing information. In some cases where the differences become part of the product description, it may be more appropriate to use a term such as *variant.*

3. The term *imperfection* is a general classification. Each imperfection type will usually be identified by its specific name (for example, scratch, weight, missing part, and so on). The severity or magnitude indicator may be a measurement deviation, a quasi-measurement deviation, a guide identification, or some other appropriate scale rating. Some imperfections may

involve a large number of severity or magnitude classifications, while others, such as a missing part, may involve only one.

4. The very existence of tolerance is recognition that achieving perfection for every quality characteristic is essentially impractical on an economic basis and, under usual circumstances, impossible in a physical sense. In many situations perfection cannot be defined other than as some desired aim which may be in the form of a single value or a sort of central core of variations. The definition may be precise in some instances, but vague in others. An imperfection may take the form of an unplanned presence or absence of some substance, a departure from the usual appearance of a product or service, or a deviation from intended physical properties or performance characteristics. As long as imperfections are of relatively low severity or magnitude and do not affect the intended use or intrinsic quality, they are customary and not unexpected in products and services. When imperfections are relatively large, either exceeding tolerances or affecting use or safety, they become of concern. The appropriate interpretations of "relatively small" or "relatively large" are derived from the stated or implied product or service requirements. (See also *blemish, defect, nonconformity.*)

Effective quality control practices usually call for making use of information related to lower-severity imperfections in order to determine trends or to detect the start of potential quality problems. (See definition and comment under *designated imperfections.*) The use of this information for control purposes is distinct from product or service release or disposition functions in that control emphasis is on the prevention, as contrasted to the segregation, of unsatisfactory quality.

incomplete block design
A design in which the experiment space is sub-divided into blocks in which there are insufficient experimental units available to run a complete replicate of the experiment. (5)

in-control process
A process in which the statistical measure(s) being evaluated are in a state of statistical control. (1)

Note:
The term *process* may represent (a) the manufacture of physical and tangible products, (b) the output of services, (c) the collection of measurements, and (d) other variations, such as paperwork.

indifference zone
Process levels located between the zone of acceptable processes and the zone of rejectable processes (that is, between the APL and RPL). (These represent processes in which the quality measures can be considered borderline and it is a matter of indifference whether these processes are accepted or rejected based on the current sample information.) (1)

Note:
A process level located in the indifference zone would represent a process that is not centered well enough that it should be limited to having only a small risk of being called unacceptable, nor poor enough that it should be limited to having only a small risk of being accepted. This contrasts with processes located in either the zone of acceptable processes or zone of rejectable processes, where the risks of making a type I or type II error, respectively, should be small. It is usually undesirable and uneconomic for a process to be located in the indifference zone rather than in the acceptable process zone. Processes located near the APL will have a higher probability of acceptance than those located nearer the RPL.

An indifference zone exists in any sampling situation, as to have an abrupt border between acceptable and rejectable process levels would require evaluating almost every item to avoid sizable type I or type II errors for levels close to the boundary line. The indifference zone can be reduced by increasing the sample size, reducing the inherent process variability, or increasing the risks of type I or type II errors.

inspection

The process of measuring, examining, testing, gauging, or otherwise comparing the unit with the applicable requirements. (2)

Note:

The term *requirements* sometimes is used broadly to include standards of good work.

inspection, curtailed

Sampling inspection in which, as soon as a decision is certain, inspection of the sample is stopped. (2)

Note:

Inspection is often curtailed as soon as the rejection number is reached, as the decision is certain and no further inspection is necessary in reaching that decision. In single sampling, however, the whole sample is usually inspected in order to have an unbiased record of quality history. This same practice usually is followed for the first sample in double or multiple sampling.

inspection, normal

Inspection that is used in accordance with an acceptance sampling scheme when a process is considered to be operating at, or slightly better than, its acceptable quality level. (2)

inspection, 100 percent

Inspection of all the units in the lot or batch. (2)

inspection, rectifying

Removal or replacement of variant units during inspection of all the units, or some specified number, in a lot or batch that was not accepted by acceptance sampling. (2)

inspection, reduced A feature of a sampling scheme permitting smaller sample sizes than used in normal inspection. Reduced inspection is used in some sampling schemes when experience with the level of submitted quality is sufficiently good, and other stated conditions apply. (2)

Note: The criteria for deciding when quality is "sufficiently good" must be defined in objective terms for any given sampling scheme.

inspection, tightened A feature of a sampling scheme using stricter acceptance criteria than those used in normal inspection. Tightened inspection is used in some sampling schemes as a protective measure to increase the probability of rejecting lots when experience shows the level of submitted quality has deteriorated significantly. (2)

Note: It is expected that the higher rate of rejections inherent with tightened inspection will lead the supplier to improve the quality of submitted product. The criteria for determining when quality has deteriorated significantly must be defined in objective terms for any given sampling scheme.

inspection level A feature of a sampling scheme relating the size of the sample to that of the lot. (2)

Note: Selection of an inspection level may be based on simplicity and cost of a unit of product, inspection cost, destructiveness of inspection, or quality consistency between lots. In some of the more widely used sampling systems, lot or batch sizes are grouped into convenient sets and the sample size appropriate to each set is furnished for a designated inspection level.

inspection lot A collection of similar units, or a specific quantity of similar material, offered for inspection and subject to a decision with respect to acceptance. (2)

interaction A term describing a measure for the differential comparison of the responses for each version (level) of a factor at each of the several versions (levels) of one or more other factors. (5)

Note: When an interaction is determined to be of sufficient magnitude, it is implied that the effect of variation within the factor is dependent upon the versions (levels) of the other factors. Because an interaction indicates a differential effect, the effects of these factors should not simply be described in terms of averages over all versions (levels) of the other factors (main effects) involved, but separately for each such version.

An interaction involving two factors (AB) is called a *two-factor interaction*; one involving three factors (ABC) is called a *three-factor interaction*; and so on.

Example:

		Factor A version			
		1	2	3	Average effect of B
Factor B version	1	10	22	28	20
	2	20	20	20	20
Average effect of A		15	21	24	

An interpretation of these results, assuming little experimental error, is that changes in version of factor *A* affect the responses when using version 1 of factor *B*, but do not affect the responses when using version 2. Also, changes in version of factor *B* affect the responses when using version 1 of factor *A* in an opposite direction to when version 3 of factor *A* is used, and so on. Note that the main effect of factor *B* would show no effect. If the results for version 2 of factor *B* had been 8, 20, and 26, there would be no interaction because the differences between the results of the two versions of *B* at each version *A* (or the three versions of *A* at each version *B*) would be constant.

isolated lot   A lot separated from the sequence of lots in which it was produced or collected and not forming part of a current sequence of inspection lots. (2)

Note: With an isolated lot, it is not appropriate to use sampling schemes involving switching rules because the lot is not related to other lots currently being inspected. If sufficient information about its production and postproduction history is known, it often is possible to use this information to determine an appropriate sample level. If this history is unknown, special attention is merited such as, perhaps, more stringent sampling.

See also *unique lot.*

isolated lots, unique lots, and lots in isolated sequences

Note: Single, double, multiple, and sequential sampling plans can be used in the inspection of isolated lots, unique lots, and lots in isolated sequences as in the inspection of a continuing series of lots. However, the interpretation of the OC curves, which are type *A*, differs as interest is centered on the one lot rather than on the longer-term risks. (2)

isolated sequence   A group of lots not forming part of a large sequence or continuous process. (2)

Note: An isolated sequence represents a group of lots submitted for acceptance inspection for which the use of switching rules in a sampling scheme would have essentially no effect on the quality of lots occurring later in the production sequence because of the small number of lots involved.

item   **1**: (object sense) An object or quantity of material on which a set of observations can be made.

2: (measurement sense) The result of making an observation on an object or quantity of material. (2)

K

---

kurtosis (γ_2 for populations, g_2 for samples) A measure of the shape of a distribution. A positive value of γ_2 indicates that the distribution has longer tails than the normal distribution (platykurtosis); while a negative value of γ_2 indicates that the distribution has shorter tails (leptokurtosis). For the normal distribution, $\gamma_2 = 0$.

$$g_2 = \frac{K_4}{s^4}$$

where

$$k_4 = \frac{n^2}{(n-1)\,(n-2)\,(n-3)}\left[(n+1)\,\Sigma(X_i - \overline{X})^4 - 3(n-1)\,[\Sigma(X_i - \overline{X})^2]^2\right]. \quad (6)$$

L

Latin square   A design involving three factors in which the combination of the versions of any one of them with the versions of the other two appears once and only once. (5)

Example:

		Factor 2 (columns)			
		1	2	3	4
	1	*A*	*B*	*C*	*D*
Factor 1	2	*B*	*C*	*D*	*A*
(rows)	3	*C*	*D*	*A*	*B*
	4	*D*	*A*	*B*	*C*

Versions of the third factor are shown by the Latin letters.

Note: Latin square designs are generally used to eliminate two block effects, not of primary interest in the experiment, by balancing out their contributions. See also *block*. The blocks are customarily identified with the rows and columns of the square. For example, the rows might be days and the columns operators. The number of versions (n) of the principal factor and of each of the block factors must be the same. The number of treatments thus will be n^2. Randomization can be achieved by assigning the versions of the principal factor at random to the letters, randomly selecting a Latin square from the listings, or by the procedures described in statistical tables such as those in Fisher and Yates, *Statistical Tables for Biological, Agricultural and Medical Research* (London: Longman Group), and assigning the versions of the block factors at random to the rows and columns of the square. (There are: 1—2 × 2; 12—3 × 3; 576—4 × 4; 161,280—5 × 5 Latin squares. Of these, there are: 1—2 × 2; 1—3 × 3; 4—4 × 4; 56—5 × 5 standard Latin squares in which the first row and first column are in alphabetical order, and from which the other Latin squares can be derived by permuting the rows and columns.)

A basic assumption is that these block factors do not interact (cause differential effects) with the principal factor under study, or with each other. If this assumption is not valid, the measure of residual error will be increased, and the effect of the factor is confounded with such interactions. The design is particularly useful, when the assumptions are valid, for minimizing the amount of the experimentation. Sometimes other principal factors are used in the block positions so that there may be three principal factors without any block factors. This is equivalent to a fractional factorial with the assumption of no interaction. Some fractional factorial arrangements form Latin squares and it may be more desirable to approach the problem from the fractional factorial viewpoint to understand the assumptions being made concerning interactions.

limiting quality level (LQL) The percentage or proportion of variant units in a batch or lot for which, for the purposes of acceptance sampling, the consumer wishes the probability of acceptance to be restricted to a specified low value. (2)

Note: The limiting quality level is sometimes referred to as the *rejectable quality level* (RQL), *unacceptable quality level* (UQL), or *limiting quality* (LQ), but *limiting quality level* (LQL) is the preferred term. When the percentage of variant units is expressed as a percent defective, this may be referred to as the *lot tolerance percent defective* (LTPD).

linear regression coefficients

1: Intercept (β_0 for population, b_0 for samples)— The parameter that indicates the average value of Y when $X = 0$.

$$b_0 = \overline{Y} - b_1\overline{X} = \frac{\Sigma X^2 \Sigma Y - \Sigma X \Sigma X \Sigma XY}{n\Sigma X^2 - (\Sigma X)^2}$$

2: Slope (β_1 for population, b_1 for samples)—The parameter that indicates the rate of change of Y for changes in X.

$$b_1 = \frac{n\Sigma XY - \Sigma X \Sigma Y}{n\Sigma X^2 - (\Sigma X)^2} = \frac{s_{xy}}{s_x^2} \quad (6)$$

linear regression equation ($\hat{Y} = \beta_0 + \beta_1 X$ for population, $\hat{Y} = b_0 + b_1 X$ for samples)

The function that indicates the linear relationship between two variables. (b_0 and b_1 are sample estimates of the population regression coefficients β_0 and β_1. $\hat{Y}$ is the average value for Y estimated for given values of X and the equation gives the regression of Y on X.) (6)

Note: The term *curvilinear regression* is used to describe the relationship (linear in terms of the regression coefficients) between two or more variables that includes estimates of curvature coefficients. Often a polynomial equation is used:

$$\hat{Y} = \beta_0 + \beta_1 X + \beta_{11} X^2.$$

The term *multiple linear regression* is used to describe the relationship between more than two variables and often takes a form such as

$$\hat{Y} = \beta_0 + \beta_1 X_1 + \beta_2 X_2 + \beta_{12} X_1 X_2 + \beta_{11} X_1^2 + \beta_{22} X_2^2 .$$

loss function   An approximation of the quality loss that occurs when an item deviates from its target value. (9)

lot   A definite quantity of a product or material accumulated under conditions that are considered uniform for sampling purposes. (4)

lot-by-lot   Inspection of product submitted in a series of lots. (2)

lot quality   A statistical measure of quality of product of a given lot. (2)

Note: These measures may relate to the occurrence of events or to physical measurements. For the purposes of this glossary, the most commonly used measure of lot quality is likely to be the percentage or proportion of nonconforming units in a lot.

lot size (N)   The number of units in the lot. (2)

lot tolerance percent defective (LTPD)   See *limiting quality level*. (2)

lower control limit (LCL)   Control limit for points plotted below the center level.

lower tolerance limit (LTL) (lower specification limit)   A tolerance limit that defines the lower conformance boundary for an individual unit of a manufacturing or service operation.

M

main effect   A term describing a measure for the comparison of the responses at each version (level) of a factor averaged over all versions (levels) of other factors in the experiment. (5)

Note: It should be noted that even though a main effect is indicated to be small, this does not necessarily mean that the factor is unimportant. Large effects of the factor may result at various versions (levels) of other factors, but may differ in sign and/or magnitude. The process of averaging in these cases would tend to make the main effect appear smaller. See also *interaction*. The term *main effect* may describe the parameter in an assumed model or the estimate of this parameter.

median (Med)   The middle measurement when an odd number of units is arranged in order of size. For an ordered set $X_1, X_2, \ldots, X_{2k-1}$,

$$\text{Med} = X_k.$$

When an even number of units is so arranged, the median is the average of the two middle units. For an ordered set $X_1, X_2, \ldots, X_{2k}$,

$$\text{Med} = \frac{X_k + X_{k+1}}{2}. \quad (6)$$

method of least squares	A technique of estimation of a parameter that minimizes $\sum e^2$, where e is the difference between the observed value and the predicted value derived from the assumed model. (5)
Note:	The experimental errors associated with the individual observations ordinarily are assumed to be independent, although the method may be generalized to the case of correlated errors. Analysis of variances, regression analysis, and contrast analysis are all based on the method of least squares and provide different computational and interpretative advantages stemming from certain balances within the experimental arrangements which permit convenient groupings of the data.
midrange	The midrange is the arithmetic mean of the largest and the smallest observed values. (6)
mixed-model analysis of variance	An analysis of variance in which the versions (levels) of some factors are fixed, but for other factors they are selected at random. (5)
Note:	Components of variance are meaningful only for the random-level factors and their interactions with fixed-effect factors.
mixture design	A design in which two or more ingredients or components must be mixed and the response is a property of the resulting mixture that does not depend upon the amount of the mixture. The proportions of each of the q components (X_i) in the mixture must satisfy the conditions $0 \leq X_i \leq 1$ and $\sum_{i=1}^{q} X_i = 1$, and each experimental point defined in terms of the proportion. (5)
Note:	In some fields of application the experiment mixtures are described by the terms *formulation* or *blend*. The use of mixture designs is appro-

priate for experimenting with the formulations
of manufactured products such as paints, gas-
oline, food, rubber, and textiles.

mode   The most frequent value of the variable. (6)

**model I analysis
of variance (fixed
model)**

An analysis of variance in which the versions
(levels) of all factors are fixed rather than random selections over the range of versions to be
studied for those factors. (5)

Note: With fixed levels, it is inappropriate to compute
components of variance.

**model II analysis
of variance
(random model)**

An analysis of variance in which the versions
(levels) of all factors are assumed to be selected
at random over the range of versions to be studied for those factors. (5)

Note: With random levels, the primary interest is usually in obtaining components of variance estimates and it is inappropriate to compute estimates of the effects of the selected factor levels.

**multilevel
continuous
sampling**

Sampling inspection of consecutively produced
units in which two or more sampling rates are
alternated with 100 percent inspection, or each
other, depending on the quality of observed
product. (2)

Note: Each period of 100 percent inspection is continued until a specified number of consecutively inspected units are found clear of variant
units. Likewise, the sampling rate is changed
after the observation of a specified number of
consecutively accepted samples.

multiple sampling   Sampling inspection in which, after each sample is inspected, the decision is made to accept
a lot; not to accept it; or to take another sample

to reach the decision. There may be a prescribed maximum number of samples, after which a decision to accept or to not accept the lot must be reached. (2)

Note: Multiple sampling as defined here has sometimes been called *group sequential sampling* or *truncated group sequential sampling.* The term *multiple sampling* is recommended by this standard.

N

---

natural process limits (NPL) Limits that include a stated fraction of the individuals in a population. (1)

Note: For populations with a normal (Gaussian) distribution, the natural process limits ordinarily will be set at $\pm 3\sigma$. If placed around the standard level, these limits identify the boundaries that will include 99.7 percent of the individuals in a process that is properly centered and in a state of statistical control.

In many circumstances (for example, several machines making the same product that serially feed into the process), it is recognized that in addition to the variability around a single level, an acceptable zone of "standard" levels (for the different machines) is required. Then the NPL may be placed around the acceptable process levels (APL) that define this zone so that the NPL identify the boundaries within which at least 99.7 percent of the individuals will be included in a process located at the APL, or inside the zone. It should be noted that there is no assumption made that the process levels within the zone are random variables. See comments under *statistical tolerance limits*.

Natural process limits will not ordinarily be the dimensional limits shown on an engineering drawing. They are mostly used to compare the natural capability of the process to tolerance limits.

nested experiment (hierarchical experiment)

An experiment to examine the effect of two or more factors in which the same version (level) of a factor cannot be used with all versions (levels) of the other factors.

Example:

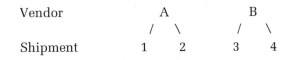

Vendor   A   B

Shipment   1   2   3   4

If two vendors are to be compared by evaluating two shipments from each, there ordinarily is no direct relationship between the first shipment of Vendor A and that of Vendor B, or similarly for the second shipment. The differences between the two versions of the shipment factor of Vendor A are nested within that version of the vendor factor and, similarly, the differences between the two versions of the shipment factor of Vendor B are nested within this other version of the vendor factor.

Note:

Generally, nested experiments are used to evaluate studies in terms of components of variance rather than in terms of differences in response levels or prediction models.

It is sometimes possible to redefine the factor into versions that can be compared across other factors, if that makes a more meaningful question. For example, shipment 1 of the previous example might represent Monday morning production and shipment 2 Friday afternoon production. The question could be framed in terms of Monday morning versus Friday afternoon production, which have a common thread, rather than in terms of two unrelated shipments. This would not represent a crossed [that is, each version (level) of a factor is used with all versions (levels) of the other factors], rather than nested, classification and could be arranged as a factorial experiment.

Vendor		A	B
	Monday	1	1
Day			
	Friday	2	2

nonconforming unit

A unit of product or service containing at least one nonconformity. (1)

Note:

See note under *nonconformity*.

nonconformity

A departure of a quality characteristic from its intended level or state that occurs with a severity sufficient to cause an associated product or service to not meet a specification requirement. (1)

Note:

In some situations, specification requirements coincide with customer usage requirements (see definition of *defect*). In other situations they may not coincide, being either more or less stringent, or the exact relationship between the two is not fully known or understood. When a quality characteristic of a product or service is evaluated in terms of conformance to specification requirements, the use of the term *nonconformity* is appropriate. The emphasis on the word *evaluated* is that of making a decision concerning conformance, whereas an imperfection rating basically deals with a measurement process. Contractual obligations, stated or implicit, may be involved, or the specification requirements may be purely internal and deliberately set tighter than the customer requirements.

For control and acceptance purposes, nonconformities are often divided into different classifications according to the degree of concern associated with the specific characteristic or group of characteristics. For example, Group *A* may include nonconformities of a type felt to be of the highest concern for the product or service. Group *B* may include nonconformities of the next highest degree of concern, and so on. For acceptance sampling plans, Group *A* may be assigned a small AQL value, Group *B* a higher AQL value than for Group *A* and smaller than for Group *C*, and so on. The classification into groups should be appropriate to the quality requirements of the specific situation.

np (number of affected units)

The total number of units (areas of opportunity) in a sample in which an event of a given classification occurs. A unit (area of opportunity) is to be counted only once, even if several events of the same classification are encountered therein. (1)

null hypothesis (H_o)

The hypothesis tested in tests of significance is that there is no difference (null) between the population of the sample and the specified population (or between the populations associated with each sample). The null hypothesis can never be proved true. It can, however, be shown, with specified risks of error, to be untrue; that is, a difference can be shown to exist between the populations. If it is not disproved, one usually acts on the assumption that there is no adequate reason to doubt that it is true. (It may be that there is insufficient power to prove the existence of a difference rather than that there is no difference; that is, the sample size may be too small. By specifying the minimum difference that one wants to detect and β, the risk of failing to detect a difference of this size, the actual sample size required, however, can be determined.)

O

observation

1: The process of determining the presence or absence of attributes or making measurements of a variable

2: A result of the process of determining the presence or absence of attributes or making a measurement of a variable. (4)

Note:

For variables measurements, the preferred term for the result usage is *observed value.*

observed value

The particular value of a characteristic determined as a result of a test or measurement. (1)

operating characteristic curve (OC curve)

1: For isolated or unique lots or a lot from an isolated sequence: A curve showing, for a given sampling plan, the probability of accepting a lot as a function of the lot quality (type A).

2: For a continuous stream of lots: A curve showing, for a given sampling plan, the probability of accepting a lot as a function of the process average (type B).

3: For continuous sampling plans: A curve showing the proportion of submitted product over the long run accepted during the sampling phases of the plan as a function of the product quality.

4: For special plans: A curve showing, for a given sampling plan, the probability of continuing to permit the process to continue without adjustment as a function of the process quality. (1)

Note: For sampling plans, the OC curve, consumer's risk, producer's risk, and so on, are used in two senses (referred to as *type A* and *type B*), depending on whether interest centers on probabilities associated with sampling from a lot of stated quality (type A), or on probabilities associated with sampling the output (series of lots, units, and so on) from a process of stated quality (type B). For sampling from a lot, the values of probabilities, risks, and so on are based on sampling from a finite population. For sampling from a process, they are based on sampling from an infinite population and the assumption that the process is in a state of statistical control.

operating characteristic curve (OC curve) (acceptance control chart usage) A curve showing, for a given acceptance control chart configuration, the probability of accepting a process as a function of the process level. (2)

original inspection The first inspection of a lot as distinguished from the inspection of a lot that has been resubmitted after previous nonacceptance. (2)

orthogonal contrasts Two contrasts are orthogonal if the contrast coefficients of the two sets satisfy the condition that, when multiplied in corresponding pairs, the sum of those products is equal to zero. (5)

Examples: 1. The following example is orthogonal.

		A_1	A_2	A_3	
a_{i1}:	Contrast 1	-1	0	$+1$	
a_{i2}:	Contrast 2	-1	$+2$	-1	
$a_{i1}a_{i2}$		$+1$	0	-1	$\Sigma a_{i1}a_{i2} = 0$ $\therefore$ Orthogonal

2. The following example is not orthogonal.

		A_1	A_2	A_3	
a_{i1}:	Contrast 1	-1	0	$+1$	
a_{i2}:	Contrast 2	0	-1	$+1$	
$\overline{a_{i1}a_{i2}}$		0	0	$+1$	$\Sigma a_{i1}a_{i2} = 1$
					$\therefore$ Not orthogonal

Note: Orthogonal contrasts represent estimators of independent questions. Unless the contrasts are orthogonal, some confounding will result. See also *contrast analysis*.

orthogonal design   A design in which all pairs of factors at particular versions (levels) appear together an equal number of times. (5)

Example: A table of orthogonal arrays derived for a half-replicate of a 2^4 factorial follows on page 83.

Note: Orthogonal designs include a wide variety of special designs such as a Latin square, a completely randomized factorial design, a fractional factorial, and so forth that are already defined or derived. It is also possible, and useful, to construct an orthogonal design by using appropriate tables of orthogonal arrays in which the sum of products of elements in any pair of arrays, adjusted by the mean of the array, is equal to zero.

Statistical analysis of the results from experiments using orthogonal designs is generally relatively simple because each main effect and interaction may be evaluated independently. However, nonorthogonal designs, which may be planned or accidental (such as by the loss of data due to missing tests or gross errors), lead to more difficult, or sometimes impossible, statistical interpretation. The degree of difficulty is dependent on the nature of the nonorthogonality. See note under *regression analysis*.

Treatment combination no.			Array no.					Treatment combinations for a	
	1	2	3	4	5	6	7	full 2^3 factorial	half-replicate of a 2^4 factorial
1	-1	-1	1	-1	1	1	-1	(1)	(1)
2	1	-1	-1	-1	-1	1	1	a	ad
3	-1	1	-1	-1	1	-1	1	b	bd
4	1	1	1	-1	-1	-1	-1	ab	ab
5	-1	-1	1	1	-1	-1	1	c	cd
6	1	-1	-1	1	1	-1	-1	ac	ac
7	-1	1	-1	1	-1	1	-1	bc	bc
8	1	1	1	1	1	1	1	abc	abcd
2^3 Factorial contrast name	A	B	AB	C	AC	BC	ABC		
Half-replicate 2^4 (or 2^{4-1}) fractional factorial contrast name	A + BCD	B + ACD	AB + CD	C + ABD	AC + BD	BC + AD	D + ABC	Aliased contrasts	

Defining contrast *ABCD* cannot be estimated

P

p

1: Used in the sense of a proportion or fraction: The ratio of the number of units (areas of opportunity) in which at least one event of a given classification occurs, to the total number of units (areas of opportunity) sampled. A unit (area of opportunity) is to be counted only once, even if several events of the same classification are encountered therein.

2: Used in the sense of percent: The percentage of the total number of units (areas of opportunity) in a sample in which an event of a given classification occurs. A unit (area of opportunity) is to be counted only once, even if several events of the same classification are encountered therein. (1)

Note: When p or the other statistical measures are used in analyses, it is customary to identify them by titles pertaining to the specific event.

$p_{.95}, p_{.50}, p_{.10},$ $p_{.05},$ **and so on**

The submitted quality in terms of the proportion of variant units for which the probability of acceptance is 0.95, 0.50, 0.10, 0.05, and so on for a given sampling plan. (2)

p_1

The percent of nonconforming individual items occurring when the process is located at the acceptable process level (APL). (1)

p₂ The percent of nonconforming individual items occurring when the process is located at the rejectable process level (RPL). (1)

Note: The $p_{.95}$, $p_{.50}$, $p_{.10}$, $p_{.05}$, and so on may pertain to either lot quality or process quality. See also note under *operating characteristic curve.*

P_p_ The performance index, identified

$$P_p = \frac{\text{USL} - \text{LSL}}{6S}$$

S = Total standard deviation.

The total standard deviation takes into account both within-lots and between-lots variation. (8)

P_pk_ The performance index that measures performance at the specification limit that has the highest chance of a part beyond the limit. Defined as the minimum (PPL, PPU). (8)

P_pm_ The performance index that takes into account the location of the mean, defined as

$$\frac{\text{USL} - \text{LSL}}{6 \sqrt{S^2 + (\mu - T)^2}} . \text{(8)}$$

parameter A constant or coefficient that describes some characteristic of a population (for example, standard deviation, average, regression coefficient). (6)

partially balanced incomplete block design (PBIB) An incomplete block design in which each block contains the same number k of different versions from the t versions of the principal factor and they are arranged so that not all pairs of versions occur together in the same number of the b blocks so that some versions can be compared with greater precision than others.

Note: The design implies that every version of the principal factor appears the same number of times r in the experiment.

Example: $t = 6$, $k = 4$, $b = 6$, $r = 4$, $n_1 = 1$, $n_2 = 4$, $\lambda_1 = 4$, $\lambda_2 = 2$

A version of the principal factor table follows.

	1	1	4	2	5
	2	2	5	3	6
Block	3	3	6	1	4
	4	4	1	5	2
	5	5	2	6	3
	6	6	3	4	1

In this design, every version occurs $r = 4$ times, and if we start with any version (say version 1), we find $n_1 = 1$ version (say, version 4) that appears together with version 1 in $\lambda_1 = 4$ blocks and $n_2 = 4$ versions (nos. 2, 3, 5, and 6) that appear together with version 1 in $\lambda_2 = 2$ blocks. These parameters n_1, n_2, λ_1, and λ_2 are the same whatever the starting version may be.

partially nested experiment   A nested experiment in which several factors may be crossed as in factorial experiments and other factors nested within the crossed combinations. (5)

Note: It is not unusual to find that experiments consist of both factorial and nested segments. See *nested experiment.*

population   The totality of items or units of material under consideration. (1)

Note: The items may be units or measurements, and the population may be real or conceptual. Thus *population* may refer to all the items actually produced in a given day or all that might be produced if the process were to continue in-control.

population means

1. Population mean μ
   a. σ known:

$$\text{LCL: } \overline{X} - z_{\alpha/2}\left(\frac{\sigma}{\sqrt{n}}\right)$$

$$\text{UCL: } \overline{X} - z_{\alpha/2}\left(\frac{\sigma}{\sqrt{n}}\right)$$

   b. σ unknown:

$$\text{LCL: } \overline{X} = t_{(n-1,\,\alpha/2)}\left(\frac{s}{\sqrt{n}}\right)$$

$$\text{UCL: } \overline{X} + t_{(n-1,\,\alpha/2)}\left(\frac{2}{\sqrt{n}}\right)$$

2. Mean difference $\mu_1 - \mu_2$ (independent samples)
   a. σ_1 and σ_2 known:

$$\text{LCL: } (\overline{X}_1 - \overline{X}_2) - z_{\alpha/2}\sigma_{(\overline{X}_1 - \overline{X}_2)}$$

$$\text{UCL: } (\overline{X}_1 - \overline{X}_2) + z_{\alpha/2}\sigma_{(\overline{X}_1 - \overline{X}_2)}$$

where

$$\sigma\,(\overline{x}_1 - \overline{x}_2) = \sqrt{\frac{\sigma_1^2}{n_1} + \frac{\sigma_2^2}{n_2}}$$

b. σ_1 and σ_2 unknown and assumed equal:

$$\text{LCL: } (\overline{X}_1 - \overline{X}_2) - t_{(n_1+n_2-2,\ \alpha/2)} s_{(\overline{x}_1-\overline{x}_2)}$$

$$\text{UCL: } (\overline{X}_1 - \overline{X}_2) + t_{(n_1+n_2-2,\ \alpha/2)} s_{(\overline{x}_1-\overline{x}_2)}$$

where

$$s_{(\overline{x}_1 - \overline{x}_2)} = \sqrt{\left(\frac{1}{n_1} + \frac{1}{n_2}\right)\left(\frac{(n_1 - 1)\, s_1^2 + (n_2 - 1)\, s_2^2}{n_1 + n_2 - 2}\right)} . \quad (6)$$

population proportions

1. Population proportion π
   a. Binomial distribution
      i. Large sample:

$$\text{LCL: } p - z_{\alpha/2} \sqrt{\frac{p(1 - p)}{n}}$$

$$\text{UCL: } p + z_{\alpha/2} \sqrt{\frac{p(1 - p)}{n}}$$

      ii. Small sample: Nomograph in Figures 3 and 4.
   b. For the hypergeometric distribution, see J. H. Chung and D. B. Delury, *Confidence Limits for the Hypergeometric Distribution* (Toronto: University of Toronto Press, 1950).

2. Difference of two proportions, $\pi_1 - \pi_2$, binomial distribution:

$$\text{LCL: } (p_1 - p_2) - z_{\alpha/2} s_{(p_1-p_2)}$$

$$\text{UCL: } (p_1 - p_2) + z_{\alpha/2}\, s_{(p_1-p_2)}$$

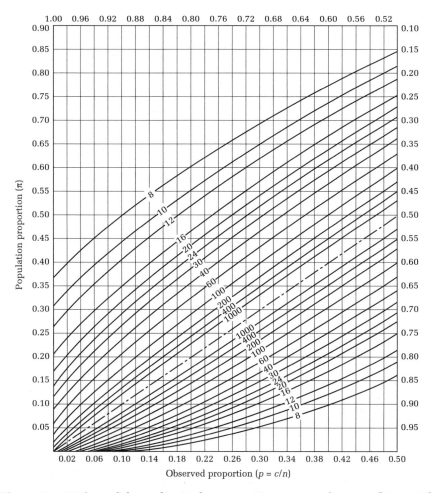

Figure 3. 95% confidence limits for proportion nonconforming (binomial distribution). Sample size *n* given by numbers on curves. Reproduced with permission from E. S. Pearson and H. O. Hartley, *Biometrika Tables for Statisticians,* Vol. 1 (Cambridge: The University Press, 1954).

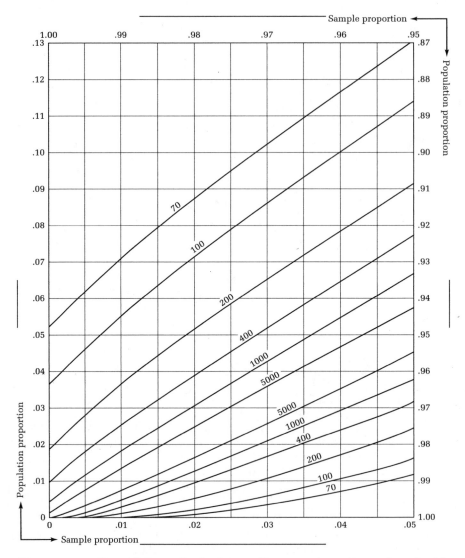

Figure 4. 95% confidence limits for small proportions. Reproduced with permission from *Journal of Quality Technology*, Lloyd S. Nelson, "Technical Aids," Vol. 13, no. 3 (July 1981): 216.

where

$$s_{p_1 - p_2} = \sqrt{\hat{p}(1 - \hat{p}) \left(\frac{1}{n_1} + \frac{1}{n_2} \right)}$$

and

$$\hat{p} = \frac{n_1 p_1 + n_2 p_2}{n_1 + n_2} \ . \ (6)$$

**population
standard
deviation σ**

$$\text{LCL: } s \sqrt{\frac{n - 1}{\chi^2_{(n-1, \, \alpha/2)}}}$$

$$\text{UCL: } s \sqrt{\frac{n - 1}{\chi^2_{(n-1, \, 1-\alpha/2)}}} \ . \ (6)$$

**population
variance σ²**

$$\text{LCL: } \frac{(n - 1) \, s^2}{\chi^2_{(n-1, \, \alpha/2)}}$$

$$\text{UCL: } \frac{(n - 1) \, s^2}{\chi^2_{(n-1, \, 1-\alpha/2)}} \ . \ (6)$$

power curve   The curve showing the relation between the probability $(1 - \beta)$ of rejecting the hypothesis that a sample belongs to a given population with a given characteristic(s) and the actual population value of that characteristic(s). (6)

Note: If β, the probability of accepting the hypothesis, is used instead of $(1 - \beta)$, the curve is called an *operating characteristic (OC) curve* (used mainly in sampling plans for quality control).

PPL   The lower performance index, defined as

$$\frac{(\overline{X} - \text{LSL})}{3S} \, . \, (8)$$

PPU   The upper performance index, defined as

$$\frac{\text{USL} - \overline{X}}{3S} \, . \, (8)$$

precision   The closeness of agreement between randomly selected individual measurements or test results. (4)

Note: The standard deviation of the error of measurement is sometimes called a *measure of imprecision.*

predictor variable A variable whose versions (levels) are selected, such as a factor level in an experiment, whether the selection is or is not in the control of the experimenter. (5)

Note: This is sometimes referred to as an *independent variable.*

probability of acceptance (P_a) The probability that a lot will be accepted under a given sampling plan. (2)

Note: See also note under *operating characteristic curve.*

probability of rejection (P_r) The probability that a lot will not be accepted under a given sampling plan. (2)

Note: The alternative to acceptance is commonly referred to as *rejection*, although in practice the alternate often takes some form other than outright rejection; for example, holding for more detailed tests.

See also notes under *operating characteristic curve* and *reject.*

process average (quality level sense)	The average value of process quality in terms of the percentage or proportion of variant units. (2)
Note:	When this figure is derived from samples, it is properly known as the *estimated process average.*
process capability	The limits within which a tool or process operates based upon minimum variability as governed by the prevailing circumstances. (6)
Note:	The phrase "by the prevailing circumstances" indicates that the definition of inherent variability of a process involving only one operator, one source of raw material, and so on differs from one involving multiple operators, and many sources of raw material, and so on. If the measure of inherent variability (see also *state of statistical control*) is made within very restricted circumstances, it is necessary to add components for frequently occurring assignable sources of variation that cannot economically be eliminated.
process quality	A statistical measure for the quality of product from a given process. (2)
Note:	This measure may be qualitative (attributes sense) or quantitative (variables sense). For the purposes of this glossary, the most commonly used measure of process quality is likely to be the percentage or proportion of nonconforming units in the process.

Q

Q (quality score)   A numerical indicator used to measure the relative quality of incoming materials, operations, and in-process or final products and service. (1)

Note: Quality scores are a quantification of relative evaluations of quality. One frequently used quality score is the weighted sum of the count of events of various classifications, where each classification is assigned a weight. The selection of the appropriate weights is complex and involves many factors that can affect the usefulness of the quality score. Such factors may include the relative importance of various event categories; the relative severity of events within a category; the likelihood that an event of a given classification will actually (rather than potentially) occur as a product or service is used under different circumstances; and so on. If the weights increase as measurements or imperfections increase in magnitude or severity, a high score would reflect relatively poorer quality, which is contrary to common expectations of a scoring system. Therefore, while it is useful to plot Q on a control chart, a quality index in which a target score is divided by the calculated score is often a more understandable number to report.

Note: In some applications quality scores are called *demerit scores*, with the weights being called *demerits.* See also *D (demerit).* In some instances an average quality score per unit (unit of opportunity) of *n* items is calculated (Q/n), such as the average score per item in a shipping unit of *n* items. For a group of *k* units, the average quality score per group is Q/kn.

quality The totality of features and characteristics of a product or service that bear on its ability to satisfy given needs. (3)

Note: In order to be able to assure, control, or improve quality, it is necessary to be able to evaluate it. This definition calls for the identification of those characteristics and features bearing upon the "fitness for use" of a product or service. The "ability to satisfy given needs" reflects value to the customer and includes economics as well as safety, availability, maintainability, reliability, design, and all other characteristics that the need for the product or service involves. The phrase "given needs" includes defining a price as well as stating what must be achieved, as it is usually possible to improve use characteristics if price is not a limitation.

Specifications for the manufacture of a product or the delivery of a service are a translation of these features and characteristics into manufacturing or performance terms. The features and characteristics often are considered in relationship to the design and specification of the product or service; to the conformance of the product or service to specifications; and to the compliance of the supplier of the product or service to requirements. This approach provides a reminder of the distinction between the functional and implemental aspects inherent in the design concept and specifications, and in the conformance and compliance aspects of the product and the implementation process.

Throughout this glossary, reference is made to *product* or *service*. These words are intended in a broad sense, but in appropriate situations it may be preferable to substitute more specific terms such as *facility, system, component*, and so on. The word *product* also is sometimes defined to include both *goods* and *services*, but that has not been done here so as to draw attention to the service aspects.

quality, relative

Degree of excellence of a product or service. (3)

Note:

The word *quality* is often used by the layperson in a relative sense that does not include many of the quantitative attributes, such as the economic aspect of given needs. Thus, a "prestige" automobile often is referred to as being of higher quality than a "production" model, even though the price difference is large. In essence, the word is used loosely in a descriptive sense to convey a comparison of selected features and characteristics and, therefore, should be modified by the term *relative*. The quality aims for the production model would include a lower price than for the prestige model, but also would include fewer features. The customer, having selected the quality that is operationally adequate and financially affordable, should compare his or her purchase to that set of requirements, whether prestige or production.

quality assurance

All those planned or systematic actions necessary to provide adequate confidence that a product or service will satisfy given needs. (3)

Note:

Quality assurance involves making sure that quality is what it should be. This includes a continuing evaluation of adequacy and effectiveness with a view to having timely corrective measures and feedback initiated where necessary. For a specific product or service, quality assurance involves the necessary plans and actions to provide confidence through verifications, audits, and the evaluation of the quality factors that affect the adequacy of the design for intended application, specification, production, installation, inspection, and use of the product or service. Providing assurance may involve producing evidence.

When quality assurance is used in the total system sense, as it normally is without a restrictive adjective, it has to do with all aspects of quality. When it is used in a more restricted sense for a particular phase or function within the total quality assurance system, the phrase *quality assurance* is modified by an adjective or used as an adjective to restrict some other operation (for example, conformance quality assurance).

quality control   The operational techniques and the activities that sustain a quality of product or service that will satisfy given needs; also the use of such techniques and activities. (3)

Note: The aim of quality control is to provide quality that is satisfactory (for example, safe, adequate, dependable, and economical). The overall system involves integrating the quality aspects of several related steps, including the proper *specification* of what is wanted; *design* of the product or service to meet the requirements; *production* or *installation* to meet the full intent of the specification; *inspection* to determine whether the resulting product or service conforms to the applicable specification; and *review of usage* to provide for revision of specification. Effective utilization of these technologies and activities is an essential element in the economic control of quality.

When quality control is used in the total system sense, as it normally is without a restrictive adjective, is has to do with making quality what it should be. When used in a more restricted sense for a particular phase or function within the total quality control system, the phrase *quality control* is modified by an adjective (for example, process quality control, manufacturing quality control, design quality control, and so on). In the same sense, it is often used as an adjective to restrict other operations to that part that belongs within the quality control system, such as, for example, quality control inspection, quality control testing, and so on.

quality management

The totality of functions involved in the determination and achievement of quality. (6)

Note:

Quality management is a part of overall management and includes quality assurance and quality control.

quality measure

A quantitative measure of the features and characteristics of a product or service. (3)

Note:

Quantitative measures may take a variety of forms, such as physical and chemical measurements, the percentage of product not conforming to specification, the percentage of product conforming to specification, a demerit index, and so on. Quality measures are used in technical applications in order to provide needed analytical information useful for control and acceptance purposes. Some are used to evaluate the conformance of individual units to specifications, while others are used to interpret quality in terms of the percentage of conforming or nonconforming units in a lot.

R

---

r　　　　The weighting factor for the current observation where $0 < r < 1$. (1)

***R* (range)**　　A measure of dispersion which is the difference between the largest observed value and the smallest observed value in a given sample. While the range is a measure of dispersion in its own right, it is sometimes used to estimate the population standard deviation, but is a biased estimator unless multiplied by the factor $(1/d_2)$ appropriate to the sample size.

　　　　　　R is computed by

$$R = \text{largest observation} - \text{smallest observation}.$$

The population estimate is derived from the following formula.

$$\hat{\sigma} = \frac{\overline{R}}{d_2}$$

Note:　　Because the range tends to be inefficient, it is not recommended that ranges be used for large sample sizes. A rule of thumb suggests a maximum sample size of 10.

randomization The procedure used to allot treatments to the experimental units so as to provide a high degree of independence in the contributions of experimental error to estimates of treatment effects. (5)

Note: An essential element in the design of experiments is to provide estimates of effects free from biases due to undetected assignable causes within the experimental space. Randomization is a process to minimize this risk. The operational procedure for assignment at random involves the use of random numbers or some similar method for assuring that each unit has an equal chance of being selected for each treatment.

randomized block design A design in which the experiment space is subdivided into blocks of experimental units, the units within each block being more homogeneous than units in different blocks. In each block, the treatments are randomly allocated to the experimental units and replicated in several blocks with a separate randomization for each block. (5)

Example: Four treatments *A, B, C,* and *D* are assigned at random to the experimental units in each of three blocks.

Block					
	1	*B*	*A*	*C*	*D*
	2	*D*	*B*	*A*	*C*
	3	*A*	*C*	*D*	*B*

Note: If the whole of the experimental material, area, or time is not homogeneous, it may be possible to stratify the material into homogeneous groups or blocks. This is one of the methods for controlling the variability of experimental units. For the completely randomized design, no stratification of the experimental units is made. In the randomized block design, the treatments are randomly allotted within each block; that is, the randomization is restricted.

randomized block factorial design

A factorial experiment run in a randomized block design where each block includes a complete set of factorial combinations. (5)

random sampling

The process of selecting units for a sample of size n in such a manner that all combinations of n units under consideration have an equal or ascertainable chance of being selected as the sample. (2)

rational subgroup

A subgroup, chosen for technical reasons, within which variations may be considered to be due only to nonassignable chance causes, and between which there may be variations due to assignable causes whose presence is considered possible and important to detect. (1)

Note:

One of the essential features of the control chart is the use of rational subgroups for the collection of data. The variability measured within subgroups is used to determine the control limits, or to verify short-term stability, while longer-term stability is usually evaluated in terms of changes between subgroups. While a relatively short time span is a common basis for a rational subgroup, other bases, such as a relatively homogeneous subarea or common conditions (for example, work by a particular operator), may be appropriate.

**ratio of
population
variances (σ_1^2 / σ_2^2)**

$$\frac{s_1^2/s_2^2}{F_{(n_1-1,\, n_2-1,\, \alpha/2)}}$$

$$\left(\frac{s_1^2}{s_2^2}\right) F_{(n_2-1,\, n_1-1,\, \alpha/2)}$$

**regression
analysis**

The process of estimating the parameters of a model by optimizing the value of an objective function (for example, by the method of least squares), and then testing the resulting predictions for statistical significance against an appropriate null hypothesis model. (5)

Note:

Regression analysis plays a role similar to the analysis of variance and is particularly pertinent when the levels of the factors are continuous and emphasis is more on the model than on the hypothesis tests. It is also useful for designed experiments with missing data, as the balance required for ordinary use of the analysis of variance is not required for regression analysis. However, lack of balance increases the order dependency (common elements are included in the first correlated term and not included in subsequent terms) of the hypothesis tests, and causes other advantages of balanced experiments to be lost. For balanced experiments, the two techniques are simply variations of the method of least squares and produce comparable results.

Example:

This example shows a designed experiment that is orthogonally balanced, say three quantitative factors studied in a 2^3 factorial, in which only a single replicate is run and the assumed model is selected as $Y = b_0 x_0 + b_1 x_1 + b_2 x_2 + b_3 x_3 + e$. This experiment yields the following regression analysis table, where $X = X - \overline{X}$.

Source	Regression coefficient	SS	DF	MS
Total	—	$S_T = \Sigma Y^2$	8	—
Constant (X_0)	$B_0 = \dfrac{\Sigma x_{0i} Y_i}{\Sigma X_{0i}^2}$	$S_{x0} = B_0 \Sigma x_{0i} Y_i$	1	S_{x0}
Regression for X_1 (A)	$B_1 = \dfrac{\Sigma x_{1i} Y_i}{\Sigma X_{1i}^2}$	$S_{x1} = B_1 \Sigma x_{1i} Y_1$	1	S_{x1}
Regression for X_2 (B)	$B_2 = \dfrac{\Sigma x_{2i} Y_i}{\Sigma X_{2i}^2}$	$S_{x2} = B_2 \Sigma x_{2i} Y_i$	1	S_{x2}
Regression for X_3 (C)	$B_3 = \dfrac{\Sigma x_{3i} Y_i}{\Sigma X_{3i}^2}$	$S_{x3} = B_3 \Sigma x_{3i} Y_i$	1	S_{x3}
Residual	—	S_E: by subtraction	4	$S_E/4$

Note: If the 2^3 experiment were replicated within the same block, the degrees of freedom for the total (line 1) would become 16 and for the residual would become 12. The residual sum of squares might then be partitioned into two elements associated with replicates and lack of fit, with 8 and 4 degrees of freedom, respectively.

The following regression analysis table serves as an addendum for the replicated experiment.

Source	SS	DF	MS
Residual	S_E	12	$S_E/12$
Replicates	$S_R = \Sigma (Y_{ij} - Y_i)^2$	8	$S_R/8$
Lack of fit	$S_L = S_E - S_R$	4	$S_L/4$

The statistical significance of each source is tested using the F statistic for the mean square of that source and the appropriate error term. For the single replicate situation, the regression terms would be tested against the residual term. For the two replicates situation, the lack of fit term would be tested against the replicates (experimental error) term to determine whether the model is inadequate, and the regression terms would also be tested against replicates. The replicates term represents a measure of experimental error free of the potential contribution of model inadequacy that would be included in the residual term.

Example: If the designed (or undersigned) experiment is not orthogonally balanced, such as having no AB response for the experiment in the previous example, a more complicated analysis and interpretation is required. The following regression analysis table results.

Source	Regression coefficient	SS	DF	MS
Total	—	ΣY^2	7	—
Constant (X_0)	$B_0 = \dfrac{\Sigma x_{0i} Y_i}{\Sigma x_{0i}^2}$	$S_{x0} = B_0 \Sigma x_{0i} Y_i$	1	S_{x0}
Regression for X_1 (A)	$B_1 = \dfrac{\Sigma x_{1i}^* Y_i}{\Sigma x_{1i}^*}$	$S_{x1} = B_1 \Sigma x_{1i}^* Y_1$	1	S_{x1}
Regression for X_2 (B)	$B_2 = \dfrac{\Sigma x_{2i}^* Y_i}{\Sigma x_{2i}^*}$	$S_{x2} = B_2 \Sigma x_{2i}^* Y_i$	1	S_{x2}
Regression for X_3 (C)	$B_3 = \dfrac{\Sigma x_{31}^* Y_i}{\Sigma x_{3i}^*}$	$S_{x3} = B_3 \Sigma x_{3i}^* Y_i$	1	S_{x3}
Residual	—	S_E: by subtraction	3	$S_E/3$

Note:　x^*_1 represents that portion of x_i not accounted for through correlation with previously computed x_i terms. The adjustment for the common element so as to remove it from the later term is usually accomplished and defined for the specific computational program used. In most standard computer programs, this is handled in connection with the inversion of the covariance matrix; in some hand computations the Doolittle method is used; in contrast analysis an orthogonalization process is followed. This process of removing the common (correlated) elements from succeeding mean squares makes the tests of significance order dependent.

In this example, all effects are correlated, but in partially balanced experiments only some are. Had the order of the effects been reversed in the analysis—x_2, x_3, x_1 (*B, C, A*)—the common element (the correlated portion) of x_1 and x_2 would have been included in the x_2 mean square rather than in the x_1 mean square, as in the example. Thus, the hypothesis testing is dependent on the order in which terms are included in the analysis. Because the regression coefficients for the assumed model should not be order dependent, the order-dependent *B* values are corrected to *b* values through a back calculation related to the previously discussed adjustment procedure. This adjustment is included in most widely used computational programs.

reject (acceptance sampling sense)　To decide that a batch, lot, or quantity of product, material, or service has not been shown to satisfy the requirement criteria based on the information obtained from the sample(s). (2)

Note:　In acceptance sampling, the words *to reject* generally are used to mean *to not accept*, without direct implication of product usability. Lots that are rejected may be scrapped; sorted (with or without nonconforming units being replaced); reworked; reevaluated against more specific usability criteria; held for additional information; and so on. Because the common language usage of *reject* often results in an inference of unsafe or unusable product, it is recommended that the words *not accept* be used instead.

rejectable process level (RPL)

The process level that forms the inner boundary of the zone of rejectable processes. (A process located at the RPL will have only a probability of acceptance designated β when the plotted statistical measure is compared to the acceptance control limits.) (1)

Note:

In the case of two-sided tolerances, upper and lower rejectable process levels will be designated URPL and LRPL. (These need not by symmetrical around the standard level.)

rejectable process zone

See *zone of rejectable processes*. (1)

rejectable quality level (RQL)

See *limiting quality level*. (2)

rejection number

The minimum number of variants or variant units in the sample that will cause the lot or batch to be designated as not acceptable. (2)

Note:

The term *variant* should be replaced by more specific terms, such as *nonconformity* and *defect*, where appropriate. The term *variant unit* should be replaced by more specific terms, such as *nonconforming unit* and *defective unit*, where appropriate.

relative frequency

Proportion of total number of occurrences to total number of members. (6)

replication   The repetition of the set of all the treatment combinations to be compared in an experiment. Each of the repetitions is called a *replicate*. (5)

Note: Because experimental error is almost invariably present, replication is required to increase the precision of the estimates of the effects. In order to do this effectively, all elements contributing to the experimental error should be included in the replication process. For some experiments, replication may be limited to repetition under essentially the same conditions, such as the same facility or location, a short time interval, or a common batch of materials. For other experiments requiring more general results, replication may require deliberately different, though similar, conditions, such as different facilities or locations, longer time intervals, or different batches of materials.

In some experiments, a pseudoreplication occurs when factors that produce no effect (average or differential) are included in the experiment. For example, two versions of a factor, such as two essentially identical brands, may be considered as replicates rather than truly different versions. When a subset of the treatments within an experiment is repeated, this is generally referred to as *partial replication*.

residual error   The difference between the observed result and the predicted value (estimated treatment response) for that result based on the empirically determined assumed model. (5)

Note: For the purpose of this definition, the term *predicted value* is understood to be the estimated treatment response determined from the empirical model derived from the data of the experiment using the assumed model. Residual error includes experimental error and assignable sources of variation not taken into account by the model. A comparison of the residual error with the experimental error can be used to assess the validity of the assumed model, as residual error may include both lack of fit and experimental error components. The variance of the residual error is usually measured in an experiment by subtracting the pooled sum of squares for terms included in the assumed model from the total sum of squares and dividing by the corresponding difference in degrees of freedom. See also *experimental Error, assumed model*, and *regression analysis*.

response surface
The pattern of predicted responses based on the assumed model derived from the experiment observations.

Note:
A sequential form of experimentation is often used in conjunction with the mapping of response surfaces in which the responses of the earlier phases are used to help predict where to select additional treatment combinations for study so as to efficiently optimize results. This approach is termed *response surface methodology*.

response variable
The variable that shows the observed results of an experimental treatment. (5)

Note:
This is sometimes referred to as the *dependent variable*.

resubmitted lot
A lot that previously has been designated as not acceptable and that is submitted again for acceptance inspection after having been further tested, sorted, reprocessed, and so on. (2)

Note:
The variant units discovered during the interim action may have been removed, replaced, or reworked.

risk,
consumer's (β)

For a given sampling plan, the probability of acceptance of a lot, the quality of which has a designated numerical value representing a level that is seldom desired to accept. Usually the designated value will be the limiting quality level (LQL). (2)

Note:

In working with an OC curve, sometimes the LQL is specified and the β risk is determined from the curve. In other situations, the β risk is specified (customarily as 10 percent) and the LQL is determined from the curve. For single sampling plans, when both the AQL and the α risk and the LQL and the β risk are specified, the plan is completely determined. (The need for n to be an integer does, however, require a decision whether to maintain the specified α or the specified β.) For double or multiple plans, the relationship between n_1, n_2, and so on must also be specified.

The risk is sometimes called the *risk of a type II error*. The exact risk depends on whether submitted quality relates to lot quality or process quality. (See also note under *operating characteristic curve*.)

risk,
producer's (α)

For a given sampling plan, the probability of not accepting a lot, the quality of which has a designated numerical value representing a level that is generally desired to accept. Usually the designated value will be the acceptable quality level (AQL). (2)

Note:

In working with an OC curve, sometimes the AQL is specified and the α risk is determined from the curve. In other situations, the α risk is specified and the AQL is determined from the curve. When both the AQL and the α risk and the LQL and the β risk are specified, the plan is determined. (The need for n to be an integer does, however, require a decision whether to maintain the specified α or the specified β.) For double or multiple plans, the relationship between n_1, n_2, and so on must also be specified.

The exact risk depends on whether submitted quality relates to lot quality or process quality. (See also note under *operating characteristic curve.*) This risk is sometimes called the *risk of a type I error.*

run

An uninterrupted sequence of occurrences of the same attribute or event in a series of observations, or a consecutive set of successively increasing (run up) or successively decreasing (run down) values in a series of variable measurements. (1)

Note:

In control chart applications; some variable measurements are treated as attributes in determining runs. For example, a run might be considered a series of a specified number of points consecutively plotting above or below the center level; or five consecutive points, three of which fall outside of warning limits.

S

σ The standard deviation of individual observations in the population.

$\sigma_{\bar{x}}$ **1:** The standard error of the average.
2: The standard error of the subgroup averages.

σ_{z_t} The standard error of the exponentially weighted moving average.

$$\sigma_{z_t} = \sigma_{\bar{X}}\sqrt{r/(2-r)}$$

sample   A group of units, portions of material, or observations taken from a larger collection of units, quantity of material, or observations that serves to provide information that may be used as a basis for making a decision concerning the larger quantity. (1)

Note: The sample may be the units or material themselves or the observations collected from them. The decision may or may not involve taking action on the units or material, or on the process.

sample (acceptance sampling sense)   One or more units of product (or a quantity of material) drawn from a specific lot or process for purposes of inspection to provide information that may be used as a basis for making a decision concerning acceptance of that lot or process. (2)

sample size (*n*)   The number of units in a sample. (2)

sampling interval   In systematic sampling, the fixed interval of time, output, running hours, and so on between samples. (2)

sequential sampling   Sampling inspection in which, after each unit is inspected; the decision is made to accept the lot, not to accept it, or to inspect another unit. (2)

Notes: 1. Sequential sampling differs from multiple sampling in that it involves individual units, whereas multiple sampling involves groups of units.

                            2. This is sometimes referred to as *unit sequential sampling* or *item-by-item sequential sampling*. Generally at the start of unit sequential sampling, a specified number of units must conform before a decision to accept can be reached.

single-level continuous sampling   Sampling inspection of consecutively produced units in which a fixed sampling rate is alternated with 100 percent inspection depending on the quality of observed product. (2)

Note: Each period of 100 percent inspection is continued until a specified number of consecutively inspected units are found clear of variant units.

single sampling   Sampling inspection in which the decision to accept or not to accept a lot is based on the inspection of a single sample of size n. (2)

skewness (γ_1 for population, g_1 for samples)   A measure of the symmetry of a distribution. A positive value of γ_1 indicates that the distribution has a greater tendency to tail to the right (positively skewed or skewed to the right), and a negative value of γ_1 indicates a greater tendency of the distribution to tail to the left (negatively skewed or skewed to the left). For the normal distribution $\gamma_1 = 0$,

$$g_1 = \frac{k_3}{s^3},$$

where

$$k_3 = \frac{n^2}{(n-1)(n-2)} \sum_{i=1}^{n} (X_i - \overline{X})^3 . \quad (6)$$

skip-lot sampling

In acceptance sampling, a plan in which some lots in a series are accepted without inspection (other than possible spot checks) when the sampling results for a stated number of immediately preceding lots meet stated criteria. (2)

specification limits

See *tolerance limits.* (1)

split-block design (two-way split-plot design)

A split-pilot design in which the versions of the second-stage factor, instead of being randomized independently within each plot, are arranged in strips across plots in each replication. Thus, it is considered as a split-plot design in two different ways. (5)

Example:

For a 3×4 design the appropriate arrangements (after randomization) might be as shown on page 114.

Note:

The design sacrifices precision on main effects (average effects) of A and B in order to provide higher precision on the interactions (differential effects), which will generally be more accurately determined than in either randomized blocks or the ordinary split-plot design. In industrial experimentation, practical considerations sometimes necessitate its use; for exam-

A_2

A_3

A_1

B_1 B_4 B_2 B_3

A_1

A_2

A_3

B_1 B_3 B_2 B_4

A_2

A_1

A_3

ple in the textile industry, factor A may be different procedures of bleaching by ClO_2 and factor B may represent rinsing by different amounts of H_2O_2 in the cooling process.

split-plot design   A design in which the group of experimental units (plot) to which the same version of a principal factor is assigned is subdivided (split) so that one or more additional principal factors may be studied within each version of that factor. (5)

Example: Three versions of factor A are tested in two replicate runs. Within each version of A, the same two versions of factor B are studied, as shown in the following table.

	Replicate I		Replicate II	
Plot				
A_1	A_1B_2	A_1B_1	A_1B_2	A_1B_1
A_2	A_2B_1	A_2B_2	A_2B_1	A_2B_2
A_3	A_3B_1	A_3B_2	A_3B_2	A_3B_1

Note: In the example, replicates serve the role of blocks to the first-stage principal factor (A) and each plot assigned to one of the three versions of A serves the roles of blocks for the additional second-stage principal factor B (within-plot factor) studies within A. Thus, the experimental error for the within-plot factor B should be smaller than that for the full experiment, if there indeed is some effect of varying the first factor. In a split-plot design, different measures of residual error are obtained for the within-plot and between-plot effects. It is possible to further extend this design in order to introduce a third-stage factor included in the versions of the second-stage factor. This type of design is frequently used where large runs or areas are obtainable from a factor whose levels are not easily changed, and the other factors can be varied readily within the runs or areas.

This type of arrangement is common in industrial experimentation, as well as in agriculture (from whence the name is derived). Frequently, one series of treatments requires a large bulk of experimental material, while another series can be compared with smaller amounts. For instance, the comparison of different types of furnaces used to prepare an alloy would need greater amounts of alloy than the comparison of different types of molds into which the alloy might be poured. The types of furnaces are regarded as the versions of the first-stage factor and the types of molds as the versions of the second stage (within-plot) factor. Another example is a large machine whose speed can be changed only by replacing the gear train, a time-consuming and expensive effort, so that infrequent changes to this factor are desired. The material manufactured at each speed can be heat-treated by several techniques, shaped under varying pressures, and smoothed using different polishing agents with relative ease of shifting from one version (level) of these factors to another. These latter constitute the within-plot factors (or second-stage factors), while the speed variations constitute the between-plot factor (or first-stage factor).

staggered nested experiment

A nested experiment in which the nested factors are run within only a subset of the versions of the first or succeeding factors. (5)

Example:

In the example for *fully nested experiment*, versions C_3 or C_4 and C_7 or C_8 might be eliminated so that factor C is studied in only versions 1 and 3 of factor B. In this arrangement, the variability of C would be estimated with only half the precision.

standard deviation

1: Population standard deviation, σ—A measure of variability (dispersion) of observations that is the positive square root of the population variance.

2: Sample standard deviation, s—A measure of variability (dispersion) of observations in the sample that is the positive square root of the sample variance.

$$s = \left[\frac{1}{n-1}\Sigma(X_i - \overline{X})^2\right]^{1/2} \text{ or } \left[\frac{1}{n-1}\Sigma(Y_i - \overline{Y})^2\right]^{1/2}$$

Note: From a simple random sample, s gives a biased estimate (underestimate) of σ.

3: Sample root mean square deviation, s_{rms}—A measure of variability (dispersion) of observations in the sample that is the positive square root of the mean square variance. (4)

$$s_{(\mathrm{rms})} = \left[\frac{1}{n}\Sigma(X_i - \overline{X})^2\right]^{1/2} \text{ or } \left[\frac{1}{n}\Sigma(Y_i - \overline{Y})^2\right]^{1/2}$$

Note: From a simple random sample, s_{rms} gives a biased estimate (underestimate) of σ.

standard error of a point on the regression line ($s_{\hat{y}}$)

A measure of the dispersion of predicted values of the dependent variable (the $\hat{Y}$ of the sample regression equation) about the population value for a given value of the predictor variable X. For simple linear regression,

$$s_{\hat{y}} = s_{y \cdot x} \sqrt{\frac{1}{n} + \frac{n(X_0 - \overline{X})^2}{n\Sigma X^2 - (\Sigma X)^2}}$$

$$= s_{y \cdot x} \sqrt{\frac{1}{n} + \frac{(X_0 - \overline{X})^2}{s_x^2(n-1)}},$$

where X_0 is the value of X for which the value of $s_{\hat{y}}$ is to be determined.

standard error of c

$$s_c = \sqrt{c}. \quad (6)$$

standard error of estimate or standard deviation from the regression line ($s_{y \cdot x}$)

A measure of the dispersion of the observed values of the dependent variable Y about the estimated average value of this variable $\hat{Y}$ over the various values of the predictor variable X:

$$s_{y \cdot x} = \sqrt{\frac{\Sigma(Y - \hat{Y})^2}{n - k}},$$

where k equals the number of coefficients estimated in the regression equation. For simple linear regression,

$$s_{y \cdot x} = \sqrt{\frac{\Sigma(Y - b_0 - b_1 X)^2}{(n - k)}}$$

$$= \frac{\sqrt{\Sigma Y^2 - b_0 \Sigma Y - b_1 \Sigma XY}}{n - 2}. \quad (6)$$

standard error of p

$$s_p = \sqrt{p(1 - p) / n}. \quad (6)$$

standard error of Q

$$S_Q = \sqrt{\Sigma w_i^2 c_i},$$

$$s_{Q/n} = \frac{1}{n} \sqrt{\Sigma w_i^2 c_i},$$

where w_i is the weight associated with each of the i categories and n is the number of items in a group of units.

$$s_{Q/n} = \frac{1}{kn} \sqrt{\Sigma w_i^2 \, c_i} \, ,$$

where k is the number of units in a group of units. (6)

standard error of the intercept s_{b_0}   A measure of the dispersion of the sample estimates of the intercept about the population value. This is a special case when $X = 0$.

$$S_{b_0} = \frac{\sqrt{S_{y,x} \, \Sigma X^2}}{\sqrt{S \, n\Sigma X^2 - (\Sigma X)^2}}$$

$$= \frac{S_{y,x} \sqrt{\Sigma X^2}}{S_x \sqrt{n(n-1)}} \cdot (6)$$

standard error of the mean

$$\sigma \overline{x} = \frac{S_X}{\sqrt{n}}$$

or

$$S_{\overline{y}} = \frac{S_Y}{\sqrt{n}} \cdot (6)$$

standard error of the predicted values (s_p)   A measure of the dispersion of individual predicted values of the dependent variable about the population value for a given value of the predictor variable. This includes the variability of individuals about the sample regression line and the sample line about the population line. For simple linear regression,

$$S_p = S_{y \cdot x} \sqrt{\frac{1}{n} = \frac{n(X_0 - \overline{X})^2}{n\Sigma X^2 - (\Sigma X)^2} + 1}$$

$$= S_{y \cdot x} \sqrt{\frac{1}{n} + \frac{(X_0 - \overline{X})^2}{s_x^2(n-1)} + 1} \, ,$$

where X_0 is the value of X for which the value of s_p is to be determined. (6)

standard error of the range

$$\sigma_R = \frac{(D_4 - 1)E(\overline{R})}{3} \; . \; (6)$$

standard error of the sample standard deviation

$$\sigma_S = S\sqrt{1 - C_4^2} \; . \; (6)$$

standard error of the sample variance

$$S_S^2 \approx S^2 \sqrt{\frac{2}{n-1}} \; . \; (6)$$

standard error of the slope (s_{b_1})

A measure of the dispersion of the sample estimates of the slope about the population value β_1:

$$S_{b_1} = \frac{S_{y \cdot x}}{\sqrt{(n\Sigma X^2 - (\Sigma X)^2)/n}} = \frac{S_{y \cdot x}}{S_x \sqrt{n-1}} \; . \; (6)$$

standard error of u or c/n

$$S_u = \sqrt{u/n}$$

$$S_{c/n} = \frac{1}{n}\sqrt{c}$$

where n is the number of items per unit.

$$S_{c/kn} = \frac{1}{kn}\sqrt{c}$$

where k is the number of units in a group of units. (6)

state of statistical control

A process is considered to be in a "state of statistical control" if variations among the observed sampling results from it can be attributed to a constant system of chance causes. (1)

statistic

A quantity calculated from a sample of observations, most often to form an estimate of some population parameter. (1)

Note:

Some statistics, such as the average ($\overline{X}$) and the sample variance (s^2), are unbiased estimators, in this instance of the mean (μ) and variance (σ^2), respectively. Others, like the range (R) and sample standard deviation (s), are biased estimators (in this instance of the standard deviation (σ)) and require a correction factor if the bias is to be removed.

Bias often is of no practical concern, particularly if it is constant and all comparisons are made on the same basis.

statistical measure

A statistic or mathematical function of a statistic. (1)

Note:

The word *statistical* emphasizes that measures are subject to inherent errors in a process and that, in estimating a population parameter, they represent a sample, with inherent sampling variability.

statistical thinking

A philosophy of learning and action based on the following fundamental principles.

- All work occurs in a system of interconnected processes.
- Variation exists in all processes.
- Understanding and reducing variation are keys to success.

statistical tolerance limits

The limits of the interval for which it can be stated with a given level of confidence that it contains at least a specified proportion of the population. (1)

Note: Statistical tolerance limits are determined from sample estimates of population parameters, with the confidence intervals reflecting the sample size on which they are based. They may involve components of both inherent and assignable sources of variability and, thus, may be based on relatively simple or quite complex determinations and assumptions.

Natural process limits are usually determined from population values or from sample estimates based on large samples (or a large number of smaller samples), and are generally set at $\pm 3\sigma$.

Statistical tolerance limits will not ordinarily be the tolerance limits shown on engineering drawings. See also *tolerance limits*.

stratified sampling   The process of selecting units deliberately from various locations within a lot or batch or from various phases or periods of a process to obtain a sample. (2)

Note: An attempt is made with stratified sampling to select known homogeneous areas within a lot that is not homogeneous: Random samples are then taken from these various locations, usually proportional in number to the size of the strata. If the strata are known, stratified random sampling will reduce the sampling variability.

subgroup   1: (object sense) A set of units or quantity of material obtained by subdividing a larger group of units or quantity of material.

2: (measurement sense) A set of groups of observations obtained by subdividing a larger group of observations. (1)

switching rules   Guidelines within a sampling scheme for shift-
                           ing from one sampling plan to another based on
                           demonstrated quality history. (2)

        Note: Rules for switching are an essential part of many
                           sampling schemes.

T

testing
A means of determining the capability of an item to meet specified requirements by subjecting the item to a set of physical, chemical, environmental, or operating actions and conditions. (3)

tests for count data (nonconformities per item)
1: (one-sample tests) If underlying distribution is Poisson, use tables of Poisson distribution [W. H. Beyer, ed., *Handbook of Tables for Probability and Statistics* (Cleveland: Chemical Rubber Co., 1966)]. If underlying distribution is not Poisson, the nature of the distribution must be ascertained, unless the sample size is large enough so that a normal test may be used.

2: (two or more independent samples) Use contingency tables. (6)

tests for means
1: Test whether the mean of the population under study, as estimated by $\overline{X}$ obtained from a sample of size n from a normal population with standard deviation σ, differs from the hypothetical or standard mean μ_0.

a. σ unknown:

$$z = t_\infty = \frac{\overline{X} - \mu_0}{\sigma/\sqrt{n}} ,$$

where z is a normal deviate (see Table 1 following the glossary section).

b. σ unknown:

$$t_{n-1} = \frac{\overline{X} - \mu_0}{s / \sqrt{n}}$$

Table 2, following the glossary section, presents t distribution.

2: Test whether the difference in means of two populations under study, as estimated by $\overline{X}_1$ and $\overline{X}_2$ obtained from independent samples of size n_1 and n_2 from normal populations with means μ_1 and μ_2 and standard deviations σ_1 and σ_2, differ from the hypothesized difference between the means $(\mu_{0_1} - \mu_{0_2})$. Ordinarily, $(\mu_{0_1} - \mu_{0_2})$ is taken to be zero.

a. σ_1 and σ_2 known:

$$z = t_\infty = \frac{(\overline{X}_1 - \overline{X}_2) - (\mu_{0_1} - \mu_{0_2})}{\sqrt{(\sigma_1^2 / n_1) + (\sigma_2^2 / n_2)}}$$

b. σ_1 and σ_2 unknown and assumed equal:

$$t_{(n_1 + n_2 - 2)} = \frac{(\overline{X}_1 - \overline{X}_2) - (\mu_{0_1} - \mu_{0_2})}{\sqrt{\left(\frac{1}{n_1} + \frac{1}{n_2}\right) \frac{(n_1 - 1) s_1^2 + (n_2 - 1) s_2^2}{n_1 + n_2 - 2}}}$$

c. σ_1 and σ_2 unknown and assumed unequal:

$$t_v = \frac{(\overline{X}_1 - \overline{X}_2) - (\mu_{0_1} - \mu_{0_2})}{\sqrt{s_1^2 / n_1 + s_2^2 / n_2}}$$

where v equals the minimum of $n_1 - 1$ and $n_2 - 1$.

3: Test whether the difference between observations from two populations obtained as pairs, as estimated by $\overline{d}$, the average of n paired differences $(d = X_1 - X_2)$ from a normal population with standard deviation σ_d, differs from the hypothetical or standard differences δ_0.

a. σ_d known:

$$z = t\infty = \frac{\overline{d} - \delta_0}{\sigma_d / \sqrt{n}}$$

b. σ_d unknown:

$$t_{(n-1)} = \frac{\overline{d} - \delta_0}{s_d / \sqrt{n}}$$

Note: These equations assume that either σ is known or that s is computed from the sample from which $\overline{X}$ is obtained.

tests for multivariate means   Matrices and vectors are shown in boldface. p variables have multivariate normal distributions with means μ and covariance matrix Σ.

1: Sample mean, estimated by $\overline{X}$, versus hypothetical mean μ_0.

a. Σ known:

$$\chi_p 2 = n (\overline{X} - \mu_0) \Sigma^{-1} (\overline{X} - \mu_0)',$$

where

$$(\overline{X} - \mu_0) = [(\overline{X} - \mu_0), \ldots , (\overline{X}_p - \mu_{0_p})].$$

b. Σ unknown (estimated by S):

$$T^2_{(v,p)} = n(\overline{X} - \mu_0)\, S^{-1}\, (\overline{X} - \mu_0)',$$

where

$$T^2_{(v,p,a_0)} = \frac{(n-1)pF_{(p,n-p,a_0)}}{n-p}$$

2: Differences in sample means, estimated by $\overline{X}_1 - \overline{X}_2$, versus $\mu_{0_1} - \mu_{0_2}$.

a. Σ_1 and Σ_2 known:

$$\chi_p 2 = (\overline{X}_1 - \overline{X}_2)\left[\frac{\Sigma_1}{n_1} + \frac{\Sigma_2}{n_2}\right]^{-1} (\overline{X}_1 - \overline{X}_2)',$$

where

$$(\overline{X}_1 - \overline{X}_2) = [(\overline{X}_{1_1} - \overline{X}_2), \ldots, (\overline{X}_{1_p} - \overline{X}_{2_p})].$$

b. Σ_1 and Σ_2 unknown and assumed equal:

$$T^2_{(v,p)} = \left(\frac{n_1 n_2}{n_1 + n_2}\right)(\overline{X}_1 - \overline{X}_2)\left[\frac{(n_1 - 1)S_1 + (n_2 - 1)S_2}{n_1 + n_2 - 2}\right]^{-1}(\overline{X}_1 - \overline{X}_2)',$$

where

$$T^2_{(v,p,\alpha_0)} = \frac{(n_1 + n_2 - 2)pF_{(p,n_1+n_2-p-1,\alpha_0)}}{n_1 + n_2 - p - 1}$$

Note: Parts *a* and *b* would replace

$$(\overline{X}_1 - \overline{X}_2)$$

with

$$[(\overline{X}_1 - \overline{X}_2) - (\mu_{0_1} - \mu_{0_2})]$$

if

$$(\mu_{0_1} - \mu_{0_2}) \neq 0.$$

3: Paired differences.

a. $\Sigma_{\overline{d}}$ known:

$$\chi_p 2 = n\overline{d}\, \Sigma_d^{-1} \overline{d}'$$

where

$$\overline{d} = [\overline{d}_1 - \delta_{0_1}), \ldots, (\overline{d}_p - \delta_{0_p})].$$

b. $\Sigma_{\overline{d}}$ unknown:

$$T^2_{(v,p)} = n\overline{d} S_d^{-1} \overline{d}'$$

where

$$T^2_{(v,p,\alpha_0)} = \frac{(n-1)\, pF_{(p,n-p,\alpha_0)}}{n-p}. \quad (6)$$

tests for proportions

1: Test whether the proportion of the population being sampled, estimated by p obtained from a sample of size n from a binomial distribution, differs from the hypothetical or standard proportion π_0. (6)

a.   If both $n\pi$ and $n(1-\pi)$ are greater than 5,

$$z = \frac{np - n\pi_0}{\sqrt{n\pi_0(1-\pi_0)}} = \frac{p - \pi_0}{\sqrt{\dfrac{\pi_0(1-\pi_0)}{n}}}$$

b. If either $n\pi_0$ or $n(1 - \pi_0)$ are less than 5, use tables of binomial distribution [W. H. Beyer, ed., *Handbook of Tables for Probability and Statistics* (Cleveland: Chemical Rubber Co., 1966)].

2: Two or more independent sample proportions. Use contingency table analysis [J. E. Freund, *Modern Elementary Statistics*, 3d ed. (Englewood Cliffs, N.J., Prentice/Hall, 1967)].

tests for regression coefficients Test whether simple linear regression coefficients of the population under study, as estimated by b_0 and b_1 obtained from a sample of n pairs of observations, differs from the hypothetical values β_{0_0} and β_{1_0}. These tests assume that (1) the response is normally distributed for a fixed level of the predictor, (2) the variability of the response is the same regardless of the level of the predictor, and (3) the predictor can be measured without error.

1: Intercept:

$$t_{(n-2)} = \frac{b_0 - \beta_{0_0}}{S_{b_0}}$$

2: Slope:

$$t_{(n-2)} = \frac{b_1 - \beta_{1_0}}{S_{b_1}} . \quad (6)$$

tests for variances Variables have normal distribution with variance σ^2.

1: Test whether the variance of the population under study, estimated by s^2 from a sample of size n, differs from the hypothetical variance σ_0^2.

$$\chi_{(n-1)}^2 = \frac{(n-1)s^2}{\sigma_0 2}$$

2: Test whether the variances of two populations, estimated by s_1^2 and s_2^2 from samples of size n_1 and n_2, differ.

$$F_{(n_1-1,\, n_2-1)} = \frac{S_1^2}{S_2^2}$$

3: More than two independent variances (Bartlett's test):

$$\chi^2_{(m-1)} = \frac{3(m-1)}{3(m-1) + \sum \dfrac{1}{v_i} - \dfrac{1}{\sum v_i}} \left[(\Sigma v_i)\, 1n\, \frac{\Sigma v_i S_i 2}{\Sigma v_i} - \Sigma(v_i 1 n s_i 2) \right]$$

where

m = number of variances, s_i^2 to be compared,

v_i = degrees of freedom associated with each s_i^2,

$1\,n$ = natural logarithm.

Note:　The probability values associated with Bartlett's test are severely affected when the underlying distribution is nonnormal, so this test must be used with caution. When the assumption of normality is questionable, G. E. P. Box suggests the following procedure for comparing the variances in two or more sets of observations.

　　1. Divide each group of observations into subgroups of equal size (perhaps three to five observations), using a suitable process of randomization.

　　2. Calculate s^2 and log s^2 for each subgroup.

　　3. Carry out an analysis of variance computation, using the log s^2 terms as the observations.

　　If the mean square among groups is not significantly greater than the mean square within groups, using the customary *F*-test, accept the null hypothesis that the variances of the original groups of observations are equal. [G. E. P. Box, "Non-Normality and Tests on Variances," *Biometrika 40* (1953): 318–35. See also O. L. Davies, *Statistical Methods in Research and Production*, 3d ed. (Edinburgh: Oliver & Boyd, 1957), 140–41.]

tests of significance

Significance tests are a method of deciding, with certain predetermined risks of error, (1) whether the population associated with a sample differs from the one that has been specified; (2) whether the populations associated with each of two samples differ; or (3) whether the populations associated with each of more than two samples differ. Significance testing is equivalent to the testing of hypotheses. Therefore, a clear statement of the null hypothesis, alternative hypotheses, and an a priori commitment to a significance level are required. (6)

tolerance (specification sense)

The total allowable variation around a level or state (upper limit minus lower limit), or the maximum acceptable excursion of a characteristic. (1)

Note:

The determination of the amount of variation to be allowed involves the product or service requirements and consideration of process capability (see *natural process limits*), measurement variability, and other appropriate elements or some compromise among these. See also *tolerance limits*.

tolerance limits (specification limits)

Limits that define the conformance boundaries for an individual unit of a manufacturing or service operation. (1)

Note:

Limits may be established either with or without the use of probability consideration. Tolerance limits may be in the form of a single (unilateral) limit (upper or lower) or double (bilateral) limits (upper and lower). Double, or two-sided, limits occur more frequently. Double limits are often stated as a symmetrical deviation from a stated value, but they need not be symmetrical.

Frequently, the term *specification limits* is used instead of *tolerance limits*. While *tolerance limits* is generally preferred in terms of evaluating the manufacturing or service requirements, *specification limits* may be more appropriate for categorizing material, product, or service in terms of stated requirements or when statistical tolerance limits are applied.

Another term, *test limits*, is sometimes used to reflect measurement error. For a prescribed testing procedure, agreement may be reached to widen the nominal tolerance limits to include a component for measurement error (consumer's responsibility) or to narrow the nominal tolerance limits to exclude that component (producer's responsibility). Normally, the nominal tolerance limits are used, and both the producer and consumer should recognize that these limits are effectively bands, rather than sharp delineations.

treatment   A combination of the versions (levels) of each of the factors assigned to an experimental unit. (5)

2^n factorial experiment   A factorial experiment in which n factors are studied, each of them in two versions (levels). (5)

Note: The 2^n factorial is a special case of the general factorial. See also *factorial experiment (general)*. A popular code is to indicate a small letter when a factor is at its high level, and omit the letter when it is at its low level. When all factors are at their low level the code is (1).

Example: A 2^3 factorial with factors A, B, and C is presented here.

					Level			
Factor	A	Low	High	Low	High	Low	High	Low	High
	B	Low	Low	High	High	Low	Low	High	High
	C	Low	Low	Low	Low	High	High	High	High
Code		(1)	a	b	ab	c	ac	bc	abc

This type of identification has advantages for defining blocks, confounding, and aliasing. See also *confounded factorial design* and *fractional factorial design*.

Factorial experiments, regardless of the form of analysis used, essentially involve contrasting the various versions (levels) of the factors.

Example: A two-factor, two-level factorial 2^2 is shown here.

$$A: [a - (1)] \qquad\qquad + \qquad\qquad [ab - b]$$
Contrast of A at the low level of B Contrast of A at the high level of B

$$B: [b - (1)] \qquad\qquad + \qquad\qquad [ab - a]$$
Contrast of B at the low level of A Contrast of B at the high level of A

$$AB: [ab - b] \qquad\qquad - \qquad\qquad [a - (1)]$$
Contrast of the contrasts of A at the high level of B
and at the low level of B

or

$$[ab - a] \qquad\qquad - \qquad\qquad [b - (1)]$$
Contrast of the contrasts of B at the high level of A
and at the low level of A.

Each contrast can be derived from the development of a symbolic product of two factors, these factors being of the form $(a \pm 1)$, $(b \pm 1)$, using -1 when the capital letter (A, B) is included in the contrast and $+1$ when it is not. Thus,

$$A: (a - 1)(b + 1)$$
$$B: (a + 1)(b - 1)$$
$$AB: (a - 1)(b - 1)$$

These expressions usually are written in a standard order, in this case:

$$A: -(1) + a - b + ab$$
$$B: -(1) - a + b + ab$$
$$AB: (1) - a - b + ab$$

Note that the coefficient of each treatment combination in AB ($+1$ or -1) is the product of the corresponding coefficients in A and B. This property is general in 2^n factorial experiments. If divided by 2, the A term represents the effect of A averaged over the two levels of B; that is, a main effect or average effect. Similarly, B represents the average effect of B over both levels of A. The AB term contrasts the effect of A at the high and the low levels of B (or the effect of B at the high and low levels of A): that is, an interaction or differential effect.

This example is, of course, the simplest case, but it illustrates the basic principles. The contrasts may appear more complex as additional factors are introduced.

type I error (acceptance control sense) The incorrect decision that a process is unacceptable when, in fact, perfect information would reveal that it is located within the zone of acceptable processes. (1)

type II error (acceptance control sense) The incorrect decision that a process is acceptable when, in fact, perfect information would reveal that it is located within the zone of rejectable processes. (1)

U

---

u or c/n
(count per unit)

The average count, or average number of events of a given classification, per unit (unit area of opportunity) occurring within a sample. More than one event may occur in a unit (unit of opportunity), and each such event is counted. (1)

Note:

Sometimes $\bar{c}$ is used instead of c/n, but it is necessary then to recognize that it is the $\bar{c}$ for the unit of n items and not for a group of k units, as would be the case for c (count).

unacceptable quality level (UQL)

See *limiting quality level.* (2)

uncertainty

An indication of the variability associated with a measured value that takes into account two major components of error: (1) bias, and (2) the random error attributed to the imprecision of the measurement process. (4)

Note:

Quantitative measures of uncertainty generally require descriptive statements of explanation because of differing circumstances. For example, (1) the bias and imprecision may both be negligible; (2) the bias may be not negligible while the imprecision is negligible; (3) neither the bias nor the imprecision may be negligible;

135

(4) the bias may be negligible while the imprecision is not negligible.

ungrouped frequency distribution   A frequency distribution based on cells consisting of only one value of the possible individual observations. (6)

unit   A quantity of product, material, or service forming a cohesive entity on which a measurement or observation may be made. (6)

Note: The entity may be a single article, a set of like articles, a set of like articles treated collectively, a subassembly, a stated quantity of material, and so on. The unit of product or service need not be the same as the unit of purchase, supply, production, or shipment.

unique lot   A lot produced under conditions unique to that lot and not part of a routine production sequence. (2)

universe   A group of populations, often reflecting different characteristics of the items or material under consideration. (4)

Note: While *population* and *universe* are most frequently used synonymously, universe is sometimes used to include a group of populations. For example, a test sample of coal may be measured to obtain BTU/lb, % ash, % H_2O, % sulphur, and so on. Thus, for a lot of coal that comprises the universe of interest, a population is possible for each characteristic measured.

upper control limit (UCL)   Control limit for points plotting above the center level.

upper tolerance limit (UTL) (upper specification limit)   A tolerance limit applicable to the upper conformance boundary for an individual unit of a manufacturing or service operation.

V

variables,   Measurement of quality by the method of vari-
method of   ables consists of measuring and recording the
numerical magnitude of a quality characteristic
for each of the units in the group under consideration. This involves reference to a continuous
scale of some kind. (1)

variance   **1:** (population variance, σ^2) A measure of
variability (dispersion) of observations based on
the mean of the squared deviations from the
arithmetic mean. (4)

Note: The population variance σ^2 equals $\int_R (x - \mu)^2$
$f(x)\,dx$ where R is the region over which the
random variable x is defined, $f(x)$ is the probability density function, and μ is the mean of $f(x)$.
The population standard deviation (σ) is the
square root of the population variance.

2: (sample variance, s^2) A measure of variability (dispersion) of observations in a sample
based on the squared deviations from the arithmetic average divided by the degrees of freedom.

W

---

warning limits   Limits at which attention is called to the possibility of out-of-control conditions, but further action is not necessarily required. (When warning limits, which are usually located inside the control limits, are used, the regular control limits are often called *action limits*.) (4)

X

x or y
(observed value)

Note: Specific observed values for variables are traditionally designated by X_1, X_2, X_3, and so on, or X_i for the ith observation. There is a recent tendency to use Y_1, Y_2, Y_3, and so on, or Y_i for observed values, or responses, to coincide with regression terminology where Y is the observed value or measured response and X is the selected setting of a factor or variable (for example, $Y = \beta_0 + \beta_1 X$). (1)

$\overline{X}_i$ The average of the ith subgroup (when $n = 1$, $\overline{X}_i = X = X_i$).

$\overline{X}_t$ The current subgroup average.

Note: For subgroups containing only one observation, $\overline{X}_t = X_t$.

$\overline{X}_0$ The standard or reference value.

$\overline{X}_0,\ \overline{Y}_0,\ s_0,\ R_0$ The value of $\overline{X}$, $\overline{Y}$, s, or R adopted as standard for
(standard values of computing the center line and control limits for
$\overline{X},\ \overline{Y},\ s,\ R$**)** control charts, standard given.

Note: These standard values may be based on $\overline{\overline{X}}$, $\overline{\overline{Y}}$, $\overline{s}$, or $\overline{R}$-bar values computed during a reasonable in-control base period, or on known or intended population values. Where a population value is known, a prime is sometimes added to the symbol or the Greek letters μ or σ are used. When σ is known and the population is normal, the center line for an s chart will be $s_0 = c_4\sigma$; for an R chart it will be $R_0 = d_2\sigma$. When μ is known, the center line for an $\overline{X}$ chart is $\overline{X}_0 = \mu$.

$\overline{X}_0 \pm 3\sigma_{z_t}$

Exponentially weighted moving average control limits.

Note:

A rule of thumb suggests that t be greater than 3.

**$\overline{\overline{X}},\ \overline{\overline{Y}},\ \overline{s},\ \overline{R}$
(average value of $\overline{X},\ \overline{Y},\ s,\ R$)**

The average for the set under consideration of sample or subgroup values of $\overline{X}$, $\overline{Y}$, s, or R. For samples or subgroups of unequal size, a weighted average is used. Formulas are shown here.

$$\overline{\overline{X}} = \Sigma \overline{X}/g$$

$$\overline{\overline{Y}} = \Sigma \overline{Y}/g$$

$$\overline{s} = \Sigma s/g$$

$$\overline{R} = \Sigma R/g$$

Population estimates: are given in the following formulas.

$$\hat{\mu} = \overline{\overline{Z}}$$

$$\hat{\mu} = \overline{\overline{Y}}$$

$$\hat{\sigma} = \overline{s}/c_4$$

$$\hat{\sigma} = \overline{R}/d_2$$

Note: When used to compute the center line and control limits for control charts with no standard given, a rule of thumb suggests that sample values from a minimum of 20 subgroups be averaged. While the correction factors to compensate for bias have been mentioned, estimates based on single samples have such wide variability that they do not play an important role in such cases unless n is large. They become meaningful, however, when used with average values based on a large number of subgroups where the effect of sampling variability is reduced.

        The estimates of σ shown in the formulas just given generally will not be numerically equal if $\overline{s}$ and $\overline{R}$ are computed from the same samples. As the number of subgroups averaged increases, the $\hat{\sigma}$ values for in-control data will tend to be closer together.

Y

Youden square

A type of block design derived from certain Latin squares by deleting, or adding, rows (or columns) so that one block factor remains complete blocks and the second block factor constitutes balanced incomplete blocks. (5)

Examples:

1. The elimination of the fourth row of the 4 × 4 Latin square yields this 3 × 4 Youden square.

2. If the columns in the example were considered as blocks (a second block factor) it will be seen that three columns from a 7 × 7 Latin square have been ignored, and the design would be a Youden square.

		Block factor 2 (columns)			
		1	2	3	4
Block	1	*A*	*D*	*C*	*B*
factor 1	2	*B*	*A*	*D*	*C*
(rows)	3	*C*	*B*	*A*	*D*
		D-del*	*C*-del	*B*-del	*A*-del

*Del indicates item deleted from the Latin square.

Z

z_α, z_β (or $t_{\infty,\alpha}, t_{\infty,\beta}$) The cutoff point in a normal distribution (z of t_∞) that defines the distance of the ACL from the APL and RPL, respectively, in terms of units of standard deviation or standard error. (1)

z_{p_1}, z_{p_2} (or $t_{\infty,p_1}, t_{\infty,p_2}$) The cutoff point in a normal distribution (z or t_∞) that defines the distance of the APL and the RPL, respectively, from the tolerance limits in units of standard deviation. (1)

z_t The exponentially weighted moving average at the present time t.

$$z_t = r\overline{X}_t + (1 - r)\, z_{t-1} = r\overline{X}_t + (1 - r)\, r\overline{X}_{t-1} + (1 - r)^2 r\overline{X}_{t-2} + \ldots \qquad [1]$$

$$z_t = z_{t-1} + r\,(\overline{X}_t - z_{t-1}) \qquad [2]$$

Note: The expansion of the first formula shows how exponential weighting serves to minimize the contribution of older data. The second formula expresses the current exponentially weighted moving average (EWMA) as the previous EWMA plus the weighted error due to using that previous value as an estimate of the current observation.

z_{t-1} The exponentially weighted moving average at the immediately preceding time interval. (1)

zone of acceptable processes   A zone around the standard or central level that includes those process levels representing processes that it is desired to have accepted almost all of the time. (The risk of rejecting a process located at the APL will be α, and will be smaller than α for those processes located inside the zone of acceptable processes.) (1)

zone of rejectable processes   A zone (or zones) of process levels located on or outside the RPL(s) that includes those process levels representing processes that it is desired to have rejected almost all of the time. (The risk of accepting a process located at the RPL will be β, and will be smaller than β for those processes located beyond this level in the zone of rejectable processes.) (1)

Statistical Tables

Table 1. Areas under the normal curve.

Proportion of total area under the curve that is under the portion of the curve from $-\infty$ to $\dfrac{X_i - \mu}{\sigma}$. ($X_i$ represents any desired value of the variable X.)

$\dfrac{X_i - \mu}{\sigma}$	0.00	0.01	0.02	0.03	0.04	0.05	0.06	0.07	0.08	0.09
-3.5	0.00023	0.00022	0.00022	0.00021	0.00020	0.00019	0.00019	0.00018	0.00017	0.00017
-3.4	0.00034	0.00033	0.00031	0.00030	0.00029	0.00028	0.00027	0.00026	0.00025	0.00024
-3.3	0.00048	0.00047	0.00045	0.00043	0.00042	0.00040	0.00039	0.00038	0.00036	0.00035
-3.2	0.00069	0.00066	0.00064	0.00062	0.00060	0.00058	0.00056	0.00054	0.00052	0.00050
-3.1	0.00097	0.00094	0.00090	0.00087	0.00085	0.00082	0.00079	0.00076	0.00074	0.00071
-3.0	0.00135	0.00131	0.00126	0.00122	0.00118	0.00114	0.00111	0.00107	0.00104	0.00100
-2.9	0.0019	0.0018	0.0017	0.0017	0.0016	0.0016	0.0015	0.0015	0.0014	0.0014
-2.8	0.0026	0.0025	0.0024	0.0023	0.0023	0.0022	0.0021	0.0021	0.0020	0.0019
-2.7	0.0035	0.0034	0.0033	0.0032	0.0031	0.0030	0.0029	0.0028	0.0027	0.0026
-2.6	0.0047	0.0045	0.0044	0.0043	0.0041	0.0040	0.0039	0.0038	0.0037	0.0036
-2.5	0.0062	0.0060	0.0059	0.0057	0.0055	0.0054	0.0052	0.0051	0.0049	0.0048
-2.4	0.0082	0.0080	0.0078	0.0075	0.0073	0.0071	0.0069	0.0068	0.0066	0.0064
-2.3	0.0107	0.0104	0.0102	0.0099	0.0096	0.0094	0.0091	0.0089	0.0087	0.0084
-2.2	0.0139	0.0136	0.0132	0.0129	0.0125	0.0122	0.0119	0.0116	0.0113	0.0110
-2.1	0.0179	0.0174	0.0170	0.0166	0.0162	0.0158	0.0154	0.0150	0.0146	0.0143
-2.0	0.0228	0.0222	0.0217	0.0212	0.0207	0.0202	0.0197	0.0192	0.0188	0.0183
-1.9	0.0287	0.0281	0.0274	0.0268	0.0262	0.0256	0.0250	0.0244	0.0239	0.0233
-1.8	0.0359	0.0351	0.0344	0.0336	0.0329	0.0322	0.0314	0.0307	0.0301	0.0294
-1.7	0.0446	0.0436	0.0427	0.0418	0.0409	0.0401	0.0392	0.0384	0.0375	0.0367
-1.6	0.0548	0.0537	0.0526	0.0516	0.0505	0.0495	0.0485	0.0475	0.0465	0.0455

−1.5	0.0559	0.0571	0.0582	0.0594	0.0606	0.0618	0.0630	0.0643	0.0652	0.0668
−1.4	0.0681	0.0694	0.0708	0.0721	0.0735	0.0749	0.0764	0.0778	0.0793	0.0808
−1.3	0.0823	0.0838	0.0853	0.0869	0.0885	0.0901	0.0918	0.0934	0.0951	0.0968
−1.2	0.0985	0.1003	0.1020	0.1038	0.1057	0.1075	0.1093	0.1112	0.1131	0.1151
−1.1	0.1170	0.1190	0.1210	0.1230	0.1251	0.1271	0.1292	0.1314	0.1335	0.1357
−1.0	0.1379	0.1401	0.1423	0.1446	0.1469	0.1492	0.1515	0.1539	0.1562	0.1587
−0.9	0.1611	0.1635	0.1660	0.1685	0.1711	0.1736	0.1762	0.1788	0.1814	0.1841
−0.8	0.1867	0.1894	0.1922	0.1949	0.1977	0.2005	0.2033	0.2061	0.2090	0.2119
−0.7	0.2148	0.2177	0.2207	0.2236	0.2266	0.2297	0.2327	0.2358	0.2389	0.2420
−0.6	0.2451	0.2483	0.2514	0.2546	0.2578	0.2611	0.2643	0.2676	0.2709	0.2743
−0.5	0.2776	0.2810	0.2843	0.2877	0.2912	0.2946	0.2981	0.3015	0.3050	0.3085
−0.4	0.3121	0.3156	0.3192	0.3228	0.3264	0.3300	0.3336	0.3372	0.3409	0.3446
−0.3	0.3483	0.3520	0.3557	0.3594	0.3632	0.3669	0.3707	0.3745	0.3783	0.3821
−0.2	0.3859	0.3897	0.3936	0.3974	0.4013	0.4052	0.4090	0.4129	0.4168	0.4207
−0.1	0.4247	0.4286	0.4325	0.4364	0.4404	0.4443	0.4483	0.4522	0.4562	0.4602
−0.0	0.4641	0.4681	0.4721	0.4761	0.4801	0.4840	0.4880	0.4920	0.4960	0.5000

(continued on next page)

Table 1—*continued*

$\dfrac{X_i - \mu}{\sigma}$	0.00	0.01	0.02	0.03	0.04	0.05	0.06	0.07	0.08	0.09
+0.6	0.7257	0.7291	0.7324	0.7357	0.7389	0.7422	0.7454	0.7486	0.7517	0.7549
+0.7	0.7580	0.7611	0.7642	0.7673	0.7704	0.7734	0.7764	0.7794	0.7823	0.7852
+0.8	0.7881	0.7910	0.7939	0.7967	0.7995	0.8023	0.8051	0.8079	0.8106	0.8133
+0.9	0.8159	0.8186	0.8212	0.8238	0.8264	0.8289	0.8315	0.8340	0.8365	0.8389
+1.0	0.8413	0.8438	0.8461	0.8485	0.8508	0.8531	0.8554	0.8577	0.8599	0.8621
+1.1	0.8643	0.8665	0.8686	0.8708	0.8729	0.8749	0.8770	0.8790	0.8810	0.8830
+1.2	0.8849	0.8869	0.8888	0.8907	0.8925	0.8944	0.8962	0.8980	0.8997	0.9015
+1.3	0.9032	0.9049	0.9066	0.9082	0.9099	0.9115	0.9131	0.9147	0.9162	0.9177
+1.4	0.9192	0.9207	0.9222	0.9236	0.9251	0.9265	0.9279	0.9292	0.9306	0.9319
+1.5	0.9332	0.9345	0.9357	0.9370	0.9382	0.9394	0.9406	0.9418	0.9429	0.9441
+1.6	0.9452	0.9463	0.9474	0.9484	0.9495	0.9505	0.9515	0.9525	0.9535	0.9545
+1.7	0.9554	0.9564	0.9573	0.9582	0.9591	0.9599	0.9608	0.9616	0.9625	0.9633
+1.8	0.9641	0.9649	0.9656	0.9664	0.9671	0.9678	0.9686	0.9693	0.9699	0.9706
+1.9	0.9713	0.9719	0.9726	0.9732	0.9738	0.9744	0.9750	0.9756	0.9761	0.9767
+2.0	0.9773	0.9778	0.9783	0.9788	0.9798	0.9798	0.9803	0.9808	0.9812	0.9817
+2.1	0.9821	0.9826	0.9830	0.9834	0.9838	0.9842	0.9846	0.9850	0.9854	0.9857
+2.2	0.9861	0.9864	0.9868	0.9871	0.9875	0.9878	0.9881	0.9884	0.9887	0.9890
+2.3	0.9893	0.9896	0.9898	0.9901	0.9904	0.9906	0.9909	0.9911	0.9913	0.9916
+2.4	0.9918	0.9920	0.9922	0.9925	0.9927	0.9929	0.9931	0.9932	0.9934	0.9936
+2.5	0.9938	0.9940	0.9941	0.9943	0.9945	0.9946	0.9948	0.9949	0.9951	0.9952

+0.0	0.5000	0.5040	0.5080	0.5120	0.5160	0.5199	0.5239	0.5279	0.5319	0.5359
+0.1	0.5398	0.5438	0.5478	0.5517	0.5557	0.5596	0.5636	0.5675	0.5714	0.5753
+0.2	0.5793	0.5832	0.5871	0.5910	0.5948	0.5987	0.6026	0.6064	0.6103	0.6141
+0.3	0.6179	0.6217	0.6255	0.6293	0.6331	0.6368	0.6406	0.6443	0.6480	0.6517
+0.4	0.6554	0.6591	0.6628	0.6664	0.6700	0.6736	0.6772	0.6808	0.6844	0.6879
+0.5	0.6915	0.6950	0.6985	0.7019	0.7054	0.7088	0.7123	0.7157	0.7190	0.7224
+2.6	0.9953	0.9955	0.9956	0.9957	0.9959	0.9960	0.9961	0.9962	0.9963	0.9964
+2.7	0.9965	0.9966	0.9967	0.9968	0.9969	0.9970	0.9971	0.9972	0.9973	0.9974
+2.8	0.9974	0.9975	0.9976	0.9977	0.9977	0.9978	0.9979	0.9979	0.9980	0.9981
+2.9	0.9981	0.9982	0.9983	0.9983	0.9984	0.9984	0.9985	0.9985	0.9986	0.9986
+3.0	0.99865	0.99869	0.99874	0.99878	0.99882	0.99886	0.99889	0.99893	0.99896	0.99900
+3.1	0.99903	0.99906	0.99910	0.99913	0.99915	0.99918	0.99921	0.99924	0.99926	0.99929
+3.2	0.99931	0.99934	0.99936	0.99938	0.99940	0.99942	0.99944	0.99946	0.99948	0.99950
+3.3	0.99952	0.99953	0.99955	0.99957	0.99958	0.99960	0.99961	0.99962	0.99964	0.99965
+3.4	0.99966	0.99967	0.99969	0.99970	0.99971	0.99972	0.99973	0.99974	0.99975	0.99976
+3.5	0.99977	0.99978	0.99978	0.99979	0.99980	0.99981	0.99981	0.99982	0.99983	0.99983

Source: E. L. Grant and R. S. Leavenworth, *Statistical Quality Control,* 4th ed. (New York: McGraw-Hill, 1972).

Table 2. Percentage points, Student's t distribution (upper-tail probabilities).

α ν	0.40	0.25	0.10	0.05	0.025	0.01	0.005	0.0005
1	0.325	1.000	3.078	6.314	12.706	31.821	63.657	636.619
2	0.289	0.816	1.886	2.290	4.303	6.965	9.925	32.598
3	0.277	0.765	1.638	2.353	3.182	4.541	5.841	12.941
4	0.271	0.741	1.533	2.132	2.776	3.747	4.604	8.610
5	0.267	0.727	1.476	2.015	2.571	3.365	4.032	6.859
6	0.265	0.718	1.440	1.943	2.447	3.143	3.707	5.959
7	0.263	0.711	1.415	1.895	2.365	2.998	3.499	5.405
8	0.262	0.706	1.397	1.860	2.306	2.896	3.355	5.041
9	0.261	0.703	1.383	1.833	2.262	2.821	3.250	4.781
10	0.260	0.700	1.372	1.812	2.228	2.764	3.169	4.587
11	0.260	0.697	1.363	1.796	2.201	2.718	3.106	4.437
12	0.259	0.695	1.356	1.782	2.179	2.681	3.055	4.318
13	0.259	0.694	1.350	1.771	2.160	2.650	3.012	4.221
14	0.258	0.692	1.345	1.761	2.145	2.624	2.977	4.140
15	0.258	0.691	1.341	1.753	2.131	2.602	2.947	4.073
16	0.258	0.690	1.337	1.746	2.120	2.583	2.921	4.015
17	0.257	0.689	1.333	1.740	2.110	2.567	2.898	3.965
18	0.257	0.688	1.330	1.734	2.101	2.552	2.878	3.922
19	0.257	0.688	1.328	1.729	2.093	2.539	2.861	3.883
20	0.257	0.687	1.325	1.725	2.086	2.528	2.845	3.850
21	0.257	0.686	1.323	1.721	2.080	2.518	2.831	3.819
22	0.256	0.686	1.321	1.717	2.074	2.508	2.819	3.792
23	0.256	0.685	1.319	1.714	2.069	2.500	2.807	3.767
24	0.256	0.685	1.318	1.711	2.064	2.492	2.797	3.745
25	0.256	0.684	1.316	1.708	2.060	2.485	2.787	3.725
26	0.256	0.684	1.315	1.706	2.056	2.479	2.779	3.707
27	0.256	0.684	1.314	1.703	2.052	2.473	2.771	3.690

(*continued on next page*)

Table 2—*continued*

v	2α							
28	0.256	0.683	1.313	1.701	2.048	2.467	2.763	3.674
29	0.256	0.683	1.311	1.699	2.045	2.462	2.756	3.659
30	0.256	0.683	1.310	1.697	2.042	2.457	2.750	3.646
40	0.255	0.681	1.303	1.684	2.021	2.423	2.704	3.551
60	0.254	0.679	1.296	1.671	2.000	2.390	2.660	3.460
120	0.254	0.677	1.289	1.658	1.980	2.358	2.617	3.373
∞	0.253	0.674	1.282	1.645	1.960	2.326	2.576	3.291
2α	0.80	0.50	0.20	0.10	0.05	0.02	0.01	0.001

(Two-tail probabilities)

Source: Reprinted by permission of the authors and publisher, from Fisher and Yates, *Statistical Tables for Biological, Agricultural and Medical Research* (London: Longman Group), Table III.

Table 3. Number of observation for t test of mean.

$\Delta=\dfrac{\mu-\mu_0}{\sigma}$	Single-sided test: α = 0.005 (Double-sided: α = 0.01)					α = 0.01 (α = 0.02)					α = 0.025 (α = 0.05)					α = 0.05 (α = 0.10)				
β =	0.01	0.05	0.1	0.2	0.5	0.01	0.05	0.1	0.2	0.5	0.01	0.05	0.1	0.2	0.5	0.01	0.05	0.1	0.2	0.5
0.05																				
0.10																				
0.15																				122
0.20										139					99					70
0.25					110					90				128	64			139	101	45
0.30				134	78				115	63			119	90	45		122	97	71	32
0.35			125	99	58			109	85	47		109	88	67	34		90	72	52	24
0.40		115	97	77	45	139	101	85	66	37	117	84	68	51	26	101	70	55	40	19
0.45	122	92	77	62	37	110	81	68	53	30	93	67	54	41	21	80	55	44	33	15
0.50	100	75	63	51	30	90	68	55	43	25	76	54	44	34	18	65	45	36	27	13
0.55	83	63	53	42	26	75	55	46	36	21	63	45	37	28	15	54	38	30	22	11
0.60	71	53	45	36	22	63	47	39	31	18	53	39	32	24	13	46	32	26	19	9
0.65	61	46	39	31	20	55	41	34	27	16	46	33	27	21	12	39	28	22	17	8
0.70	53	40	34	28	17	47	35	30	24	14	40	29	24	19	10	34	24	19	15	8
0.75	47	36	30	25	16	42	31	27	21	13	35	26	21	16	9	30	21	17	13	7
0.80	41	32	27	22	14	37	28	24	19	12	31	23	19	15	9	27	19	15	12	6
0.85	37	29	24	20	13	33	25	21	17	11	28	20	17	13	8	24	17	14	11	6
0.90	34	26	22	18	12	30	23	19	16	10	25	19	15	12	7	21	15	13	10	5
0.95	31	24	20	17	11	27	21	18	14	9	23	17	14	11	7	19	14	12	9	5
1.00	28	22	19	16	10	25	19	16	13	9	21	16	13	10	6	18	13	11	8	5

Level of t test. In each group the first α value is for the single-sided test and the second for the double-sided test.

1.1	24	19	16	14	9	21	16	14	12	8	18	13	11	9	6	15	11	9	7	1.1
1.2	21	16	14	12	8	18	14	12	10	7	15	12	10	8	5	13	10	8	6	1.2
1.3	18	15	13	11	8	16	13	11	9	6	14	10	9	7		11	8	7	6	1.3
1.4	16	13	12	10	7	14	11	10	9	6	12	9	8	7		10	8	7	5	1.4
1.5	15	12	11	9	7	13	10	9	8	6	11	8	7	6		9	7	6		1.5
1.6	13	11	10	8	6	12	10	9	7	5	10	8	7	6		8	6	6		1.6
1.7	12	10	9	8	6	11	9	8	7		9	7	6	5		8	6	5		1.7
1.8	12	10	9	8	6	10	8	7	7		8	7	6			7	6			1.8
1.9	11	9	8	7	6	10	8	7	6		8	6	6			7	5			1.9
2.0	10	8	8	7	5	9	8	7	6		7	6	5			6				2.0
2.1	10	8	7	7		8	7	6	6		7	6				6				2.1
2.2	9	8	7	6		8	7	6	5		7	5				6				2.2
2.3	9	7	7	6		8	7	6			6					5				2.3
2.4	8	7	7	6		7	6	6			6									2.4
2.5	8	7	6	6		7	6	5			6									2.5
3.0	7	6	6	5		6	6				5									3.0
3.5	6	5	5			5	5													3.5
4.0	6	5																		4.0

Source: O. L. Davies, "Design and Analysis of Industrial Experiments" (London: Oliver and Boyd, 1956) and "Research," Vol. 1 (Butterworth Scientific Publications, 1948).

Table 4. Number of observations for t test of difference between two means.

	Level of t test																			
Single-sided test	α = 0.005					α = 0.01					α = 0.025					α = 0.05				
Double-sided test	α = 0.01					α = 0.02					α = 0.05					α = 0.1				
Value of $\Delta = \dfrac{\mu_1 - \mu_2}{\sigma}$ / β =	0.01	0.05	0.1	0.2	0.5	0.01	0.05	0.1	0.2	0.5	0.01	0.05	0.1	0.2	0.5	0.01	0.05	0.1	0.2	0.5
0.05																				
0.10																				
0.15																				
0.20																				137
0.25															124					88
0.30										123					87					61
0.35					110					90				130	64				102	45
0.40					85				128	70			133	100	50		137	108	78	35
0.45				118	68			131	101	55		130	105	79	39		108	86	62	28
0.50			122	96	55		128	106	82	45		106	86	64	32	128	88	70	51	23
0.55		120	101	79	46		106	88	68	38	123	88	71	53	27	106	73	58	42	19
0.60	136	101	85	67	39	123	90	74	58	32	104	74	60	45	23	89	61	49	36	16
0.65	116	87	73	57	34	104	77	64	49	27	88	63	51	39	20	76	52	42	30	14
0.70	100	75	63	50	29	90	66	55	43	24	76	55	44	34	17	66	45	36	26	12
0.75	88	66	55	44	26	79	58	48	38	21	67	48	39	29	15	57	40	32	23	11
0.80	77	58	49	39	23	70	51	43	33	19	59	42	34	26	14	50	35	28	21	10
0.85	69	51	43	35	21	62	46	38	30	17	52	37	31	23	12	45	31	25	18	9
0.90	62	46	39	31	19	55	41	34	27	15	47	34	27	21	11	40	28	22	16	8
0.95	55	42	35	28	17	50	37	31	24	14	42	30	25	19	10	36	25	20	15	7
1.00	50	38	32	26	15	45	33	28	22	13	38	27	23	17	9	33	23	18	14	7

1.1	42	32	27	22	13	38	28	23	19	11	32	23	19	14	8	27	19	15	12	6	1.1
1.2	36	27	23	18	11	32	24	20	16	9	27	20	16	12	7	23	16	13	10	5	1.2
1.3	31	23	20	16	10	28	21	17	14	8	23	17	14	11	6	20	14	11	9	5	1.3
1.4	27	20	17	14	9	24	18	15	12	8	20	15	12	10	6	17	12	10	8	4	1.4
1.5	24	18	15	13	8	21	16	14	11	7	18	13	11	9	5	15	11	9	7	4	1.5
1.6	21	16	14	11	7	19	14	12	10	6	16	12	10	8	5	14	10	8	6	4	1.6
1.7	19	15	13	10	7	17	13	11	9	6	14	11	9	7	4	12	9	7	6	3	1.7
1.8	17	13	11	10	6	15	12	10	8	5	13	10	8	6	4	11	8	7	5		1.8
1.9	16	12	11	9	6	14	11	9	8	5	12	9	7	6	4	10	7	6	5		1.9
2.0	14	11	10	8	6	13	10	9	7	5	11	8	7	6	4	9	7	6	4		2.0
2.1	13	10	9	8	5	12	9	8	6	5	10	8	6	5	3	8	6	5	4		2.1
2.2	12	10	8	7	5	11	9	7	6	4	9	7	6	5		8	6	5	4		2.2
2.3	11	9	8	7	5	10	8	7	6	4	9	7	6	5		7	5	5	4		2.3
2.4	11	9	8	6	5	10	8	7	6	4	8	6	5	4		7	5	4	4		2.4
2.5	10	8	7	6	4	9	7	6	5	4	8	6	5	4		6	5	4	3		2.5
3.0	8	6	6	5	4	7	6	5	4	3	6	5	4	4		5	4	3			3.0
3.5	6	5	4	4	3	6	5	4	4		5	4	3			4	3				3.5
4.0	6	5	4	4		5	4	3			4	3				4					4.0

Source: O. L. Davies, *Design and Analysis of Industrial Experiments* (London: Oliver and Boyd, 1956) and *Research,* Vol. 1 (Butterworth Scientific Publications, 1948).

Table 5. Number of observations required for the comparison of a population variance with a standard value using the chi-square test.

v	$\alpha = 0.01$				$\alpha = 0.05$			
1	42,240	1,687	420.2	14.58	25,450	977.0	243.3	8.444
2	458.2	89.75	43.71	63.644	298.1	58.40	28.43	4.322
3	98.70	32.24	19.41	4.795	68.05	22.21	13.37	3.303
4	44.69	18.68	12.48	3.955	31.93	13.35	9.920	2.826
5	27.22	13.17	9.369	3.467	19.97	9.665	6.875	2.544
6	19.28	10.28	7.628	3.144	14.44	7.699	5.713	2.354
7	14.91	8.524	6.521	2.911	11.35	6.491	4.965	2.217
8	12.20	7.352	5.757	2.736	9.418	5.675	4.444	2.112
9	10.38	6.516	5.198	2.597	8.103	5.088	4.059	2.028
10	9.072	5.890	4.770	2.484	7.156	4.646	3.763	1.960
12	7.343	5.017	4.159	2.312	5.889	4.023	3.335	1.854
15	5.847	4.211	3.578	2.132	4.780	3.442	2.925	1.743
20	4.548	3.462	3.019	1.943	3.802	2.895	2.524	1.624
24	2.959	3.104	2.745	1.842	3.354	2.630	2.326	1.560
30	3.403	2.752	2.471	1.735	2.927	2.367	2.125	1.492
40	2.874	2.403	2.192	1.619	2.516	2.103	1.919	1.418
60	2.358	2.046	1.902	1.490	2.110	1.831	1.702	1.333
120	1.829	1.661	1.580	1.332	1.686	1.532	1.457	1.228
∞	1.000	1.000	1.000	1.000	1.000	1.000	1.000	1.000

Note: The tabular entries show the value of the ratio R population variance σ_1^2 to a standard variance σ_0^2 which is undetected with probability β in a χ^2 test at significance level of α of an estimate s_1^2 based on v degrees of freedom.

Examples: *Testing for an increase in variance.* Let $\alpha = 0.05$, $\beta = 0.01$, and $R = 4$. Entering the table with these values, it is found that the value 4 occurs between the rows corresponding to $v = 15$ and $v = 20$. Using rough interpolation, it is indicated that the estimate of variance should be based on 19 degrees of freedom.

Testing for a decrease in variance. Let $\alpha = 0.05$, $\beta = 0.01$, and $R = 0.33$. The table is entered with $\alpha' = \beta = 0.01$, $\beta' = \alpha = 0.05$, and $R' = 1/R = 3$. It is found that the value 3 occurs between the rows corresponding to $v = 24$ and $v = 30$. Using rough interpolation, it is indicated that the estimate of variance should be based on 26 degrees of freedom.

Source: O. L. Davies, *Design and Analysis of Industrial Experiments* (London: Oliver and Boyd, 1956); Eisenhart, Hastay, and Wallis, *Selected Techniques of Statistical Analysis* (New York: McGraw-Hill, 1947).

Table 6. Number of observations required for the comparison of two population variances using the F test.

The entries in this table show the value of the ratio R of two population variances σ_2^2/σ_1^2 that remains undetected with probability β in a variance-ratio test at significance level α of the ratio s_2^2/s_1^2 of estimates of two variances, both being based on v degrees of freedom.

	$\alpha = 0.01$				$\alpha = 0.05$				$\alpha = 0.5$			
v	$\beta = 0.01$	$\beta = 0.05$	$\beta = 0.1$	$\beta = 0.5$	$\beta = 0.01$	$\beta = 0.05$	$\beta = 0.1$	$\beta = 0.5$	$\beta = 0.01$	$\beta = 0.05$	$\beta = 0.1$	$\beta = 0.5$
1	16,420,000	654,200	161,500	4052	654,200	26,070	6,436	161.5	4,052	161.5	39.85	1.000
2	9,000	1,881	891.0	99.00	1,881	361.0	171.0	19.00	99.00	19.00	9.000	1.000
3	867.7	273.3	158.8	29.46	273.3	86.06	50.01	9.277	29.46	9.277	5.391	1.000
4	255.3	102.1	65.62	15.98	102.1	40.81	26.24	6.388	15.98	6.388	4.108	1.000
5	120.3	55.39	37.87	10.97	55.39	25.51	17.44	5.050	10.97	5.050	3.453	1.000
6	71.67	36.27	25.86	8.466	36.27	18.35	13.09	4.284	8.466	4.284	3.056	1.000
7	48.90	26.48	19.47	6.993	26.48	14.34	10.55	3.787	6.993	3.787	2.786	1.000
8	36.35	20.73	15.61	6.029	20.73	11.82	8.902	3.438	6.029	3.438	2.589	1.000
9	28.63	17.01	13.06	5.351	17.01	10.11	7.757	3.179	5.351	3.179	2.440	1.000
10	23.51	14.44	11.26	4.849	14.44	8.870	6.917	2.978	4.849	2.978	2.323	1.000
12	17.27	11.16	8.923	4.155	11.16	7.218	5.769	2.687	4.155	2.687	2.147	1.000
15	12.41	8.466	6.946	3.522	8.466	5.777	4.740	2.404	3.522	2.404	1.972	1.000
20	8.630	6.240	5.270	2.938	6.240	4.512	3.810	2.124	2.938	2.124	1.794	1.000
24	7.071	5.275	4.526	2.659	5.275	3.935	3.376	1.984	2.659	1.984	1.702	1.000
30	5.693	4.392	3.833	2.386	4.392	3.389	2.957	1.841	2.386	1.841	1.606	1.000
40	4.470	3.579	3.183	2.114	3.579	2.866	2.549	1.693	2.114	1.693	1.506	1.000
60	3.372	2.817	2.562	1.836	2.817	2.354	2.141	1.534	1.836	1.534	1.396	1.000
120	2.350	2.072	1.939	1.533	2.072	1.828	1.710	1.352	1.533	1.352	1.265	1.000
∞	1.000	1.000	1.000	1.000	1.000	1.000	1.000	1.000	1.000	1.000	1.000	1.000

Source: O. L. Davies, Design and Analysis of Industrial Experiments (London: Oliver and Boyd, 1956); Eisenhart, Hastay and Wallis, Selected Techniques of Statistical Analysis (New York: McGraw-Hill, 1947).

Table 7. Factors for control charts for variables $\overline{X}$, $\overline{Y}$, s, R: Normal universe factors for computing central lines and 3σ control limits.

| Observations in sample, n | Chart for averages | | | Chart for standard deviations | | | | | | Chart for ranges | | | | | | |
| | Factors for control limits | | | Factors for central line | | Factors for control limits | | | | Factors for central line | | | Factors for control limits | | | |
	A	A_2	A_3	c_4	$1/c_4$	B_3	B_4	B_5	B_6	d_2	$1/d_2$	d_3	D_1	D_2	D_3	D_4
2	2.121	1.880	2.659	0.7979	1.2533	0	3.267	0	2.606	1.128	0.8865	0.853	0	3.686	0	3.267
3	1.732	1.023	1.954	0.8862	1.1284	0	2.568	0	2.276	1.693	0.5907	0.888	0	4.358	0	2.574
4	1.500	0.729	1.628	0.9213	1.0854	0	2.266	0	2.088	2.059	0.4857	0.880	0	4.698	0	2.282
5	1.342	0.577	1.427	0.9400	1.0638	0	2.089	0	1.964	2.326	0.4299	0.864	0	4.918	0	2.114
6	1.225	0.483	1.287	0.9515	1.0510	0.030	1.970	0.029	1.874	2.534	0.3946	0.848	0	5.078	0	2.004
7	1.134	0.419	1.182	0.9594	1.0423	0.118	1.882	0.113	1.806	2.704	0.3698	0.833	0.204	5.204	0.076	1.924
8	1.061	0.373	1.099	0.9650	1.0363	0.185	1.815	0.179	1.751	2.847	0.3512	0.820	0.388	5.306	0.136	1.864
9	1.000	0.337	1.032	0.9693	1.0317	0.239	1.761	0.232	1.707	2.970	0.3367	0.808	0.547	5.393	0.184	1.816
10	0.949	0.308	0.975	0.9727	1.0281	0.284	1.716	0.276	1.669	3.078	0.3249	0.797	0.687	5.469	0.223	1.777
11	0.905	0.285	0.927	0.9754	1.0252	0.321	1.679	0.313	1.637	3.173	0.3152	0.787	0.811	5.535	0.256	1.744
12	0.866	0.266	0.886	0.9776	1.0229	0.354	1.646	0.346	1.610	3.258	0.3069	0.778	0.922	5.594	0.283	1.717
13	0.832	0.249	0.850	0.9794	1.0210	0.382	1.618	0.374	1.585	3.336	0.2998	0.770	1.025	5.647	0.307	1.693
14	0.802	0.235	0.817	0.9810	1.0194	0.406	1.594	0.399	1.563	3.407	0.2935	0.763	1.118	5.696	0.328	1.672
15	0.775	0.223	0.789	0.9823	1.0180	0.428	1.572	0.421	1.544	3.472	0.2880	0.756	1.203	5.741	0.347	1.653
16	0.750	0.212	0.763	0.9835	1.0168	0.448	1.552	0.440	1.526	3.532	0.2831	0.750	1.282	5.782	0.363	1.637
17	0.728	0.203	0.739	0.9845	1.0157	0.466	1.534	0.458	1.511	3.588	0.2787	0.744	1.356	5.820	0.378	1.622
18	0.707	0.194	0.718	0.9854	1.0148	0.482	1.518	0.475	1.496	3.640	0.2747	0.739	1.424	5.856	0.391	1.608
19	0.688	0.187	0.698	0.9862	1.0140	0.497	1.503	0.490	1.483	3.689	0.2711	0.734	1.487	5.891	0.403	1.597

20	0.671	0.180	0.680	0.9869	1.0133	0.510	1.490	0.504	1.470	3.735	0.2677	0.729	1.549	5.921	0.415	1.585
21	0.655	0.173	0.663	0.9876	1.0126	0.523	1.477	0.516	1.459	3.778	0.2647	0.724	1.605	5.951	0.425	1.575
22	0.640	0.167	0.647	0.9882	1.0119	0.534	1.466	0.528	1.448	3.819	0.2618	0.720	1.659	5.979	0.434	1.566
23	0.626	0.162	0.633	0.9887	1.0114	0.545	1.455	0.539	1.438	3.858	0.2592	0.716	1.710	6.006	0.443	1.557
24	0.612	0.157	0.619	0.9892	1.0109	0.555	1.445	0.549	1.429	3.895	0.2567	0.712	1.759	6.031	0.451	1.548
25	0.600	0.153	0.606	0.9896	1.0105	0.565	1.435	0.559	1.420	3.931	0.2544	0.708	1.806	6.056	0.459	1.541

Note: Formulas for Shewhart charts start on page 36.

For $n > 25$,

$$A = \frac{3}{\sqrt{n}}, \ A_3 = \frac{3}{C_4\sqrt{n}}, \ C_4 \approx \frac{4(n - 1)}{4n - 3},$$

$$B_3 = 1 - \frac{3}{C_4\sqrt{2(n - 1)}}, \ B_4 = 1 + \frac{3}{C_4\sqrt{2(n - 1)}},$$

$$B_5 = C_4 - \frac{3}{\sqrt{2(n - 1)}}, \ B_6 = C_4 + \frac{3}{\sqrt{2(n - 1)}}.$$

Those who prefer to define the sample standard deviation as

$$\sqrt{\exists(X - \bar{X})^2}$$

are referred to the replaced ASQC standard A1-1971 for the values of the factors C_2, A_1, B_2, and E_1 that are used for such a definition.

Table 7—*continued*

While factors are given for limits involving the range for $n > 10$, the use of the range is not recommended for sample sizes that large.

For use with control charts for individuals, factors $E_2 = 3/d_2$ and $E_3 = 3/c_4$ are given for sample sizes to $n = 10$, as shown in the following table.

n	2	3	4	5	6	7	8	9	10
E_2	2.660	1.772	1.457	1.290	1.184	1.109	1.054	1.010	0.975
E_3	3.760	3.385	3.256	3.191	3.153	3.129	3.109	3.095	3.084

A normal (Gaussian) distribution is assumed for most variables' control chart applications, and departures from this assumption affect the probability (risk) statements. The factors were derived using an assumption of normality. Because most control limits are used as empirical guides to making decisions, rather than as exact probabilistic criteria, reasonably small departures from normality should not be of concern. A more critical assumption is that all of the data are collected from a single population, as all sample and population estimates would lose meaning otherwise. Periodic checks on the continuing validity of these assumptions may be advisable.

Reprinted by permission of the American Society for Testing and Materials, from ASTM-STP 15D.

Table 8. Random orderings of numbers 1–9.

---

5 5 6 7 1	4 3 3 7 3	8 7 4 6 3	9 7 4 9 4	9 2 2 8 8	2 7 9 3 5	8 3 1 9 4
4 1 2 8 2	7 1 1 2 9	9 5 7 8 2	8 9 3 6 6	1 7 7 2 4	4 8 5 7 3	3 7 4 5 6
9 3 3 2 9	8 8 8 4 5	2 4 6 1 6	3 6 7 7 8	7 4 4 7 1	7 3 2 8 6	6 1 2 2 2
7 9 7 4 3	5 5 2 9 2	1 6 5 3 5	7 8 5 1 9	5 1 9 1 3	6 5 1 4 9	2 9 8 7 8
1 6 9 6 5	6 9 4 3 6	4 3 9 2 9	5 1 8 2 3	8 3 3 3 2	8 9 6 1 2	4 5 7 6 9
6 4 4 3 6	2 4 6 8 1	7 9 3 4 1	6 2 6 4 2	2 9 8 5 9	9 2 4 2 8	9 6 9 8 1
8 7 8 1 7	1 2 5 6 8	3 1 2 9 8	4 4 1 8 7	6 5 1 6 7	5 4 3 5 1	1 4 3 1 7
3 2 1 9 4	3 6 7 5 7	6 8 8 7 7	2 5 9 5 1	3 8 5 4 6	3 6 7 9 4	5 2 5 4 5
2 8 5 5 8	9 7 9 1 4	5 2 1 5 4	1 3 2 3 5	4 6 6 9 5	1 1 8 6 7	7 8 6 3 3
7 4 6 1 5	9 2 2 2 9	2 8 1 7 3	2 4 2 1 9	2 4 8 3 1	2 6 5 4 8	8 4 9 4 2
9 3 8 3 2	1 1 1 9 8	9 4 9 5 4	8 8 8 8 6	7 7 5 4 6	5 3 2 7 6	9 3 8 2 1
1 6 3 4 7	6 5 8 4 5	6 1 7 1 9	5 2 5 6 3	8 5 7 5 5	6 9 9 8 1	3 6 7 9 7
6 8 2 8 4	4 8 7 8 6	5 7 5 4 5	9 6 7 5 8	5 9 9 7 7	8 5 3 3 5	6 9 4 6 9
4 1 4 7 8	2 3 9 3 4	4 2 2 3 6	4 7 4 2 5	6 3 3 6 9	1 7 8 5 4	4 5 2 1 4
2 9 1 9 3	7 9 6 6 2	1 6 4 6 1	7 9 9 7 4	1 8 4 1 8	9 2 7 9 3	1 8 3 5 5
5 5 5 5 1	3 7 4 7 7	8 5 8 9 2	1 5 1 3 2	9 6 2 8 4	3 8 1 1 9	5 7 1 3 3
8 2 9 2 9	8 6 5 5 3	7 9 6 8 8	3 1 6 9 7	4 1 6 9 3	4 4 6 6 2	7 2 6 8 8
3 7 7 6 6	5 4 3 1 1	3 3 3 2 7	6 3 3 4 1	3 2 1 2 2	7 1 4 2 7	2 1 5 7 6
9 7 7 5 5	9 9 9 3 8	9 8 6 1 7	5 8 6 1 2	1 9 8 3 3	3 1 7 7 3	7 6 6 5 5
3 8 1 7 2	6 2 7 1 6	4 1 3 4 2	3 6 2 4 3	2 6 1 2 8	8 8 6 2 7	8 9 7 4 7
4 3 4 2 7	7 3 1 7 2	1 5 4 8 6	6 2 1 6 1	7 8 5 1 7	5 9 1 3 6	3 1 2 3 1
5 9 2 8 3	3 7 5 8 9	2 9 1 7 1	2 3 8 3 4	3 5 9 9 9	7 2 3 4 1	5 7 1 7 8
1 6 5 1 1	5 6 4 4 1	7 3 7 2 3	4 7 3 8 8	9 3 2 5 6	6 6 9 5 9	9 8 9 1 2
6 2 8 3 6	8 4 6 2 5	5 2 2 6 8	9 1 7 5 6	4 7 4 6 4	1 7 4 6 4	1 2 8 8 6
2 4 9 6 4	1 8 3 5 4	3 6 5 9 4	8 5 9 7 9	8 1 6 8 1	4 5 5 9 5	2 4 5 9 4
8 5 6 9 9	2 5 2 6 7	8 7 8 3 9	1 9 4 2 5	6 4 7 4 5	2 3 2 8 2	6 3 3 2 3
7 1 3 4 8	4 1 8 9 3	6 4 9 5 5	7 4 5 9 7	5 2 3 7 2	9 4 8 1 8	4 5 4 6 9
7 4 9 8 7	9 7 1 7 1	9 2 3 8 7	7 8 5 3 5	5 1 6 4 9	7 8 6 1 8	2 9 7 3 4
5 6 1 1 2	6 4 6 1 4	5 9 1 2 8	2 4 6 8 7	7 3 7 6 1	5 1 7 4 1	9 3 4 7 7
4 9 3 5 6	1 1 8 4 8	3 5 4 9 3	3 6 1 2 3	2 6 8 7 7	4 5 3 8 5	8 5 9 5 1
3 3 2 2 8	5 2 3 2 2	7 3 8 6 9	4 1 8 6 1	1 9 2 3 6	3 9 5 7 7	1 2 8 1 2
2 1 4 9 4	4 6 2 8 3	2 7 6 5 1	5 7 3 1 2	9 8 4 1 3	6 3 1 2 9	6 1 5 8 8
9 7 5 4 5	3 9 7 9 9	1 4 2 3 4	6 9 7 4 4	3 2 5 2 2	8 4 2 6 3	5 6 3 6 3
6 2 6 3 9	8 8 5 5 5	8 6 7 7 2	9 3 4 5 8	8 7 9 9 4	9 2 4 9 4	4 8 1 2 9
8 5 8 7 1	2 3 9 3 7	4 1 5 1 5	8 5 9 7 6	4 5 3 5 8	1 6 8 5 2	3 4 6 4 5
1 8 7 6 3	7 5 4 6 6	6 8 9 4 6	1 2 2 9 9	6 4 1 8 5	2 7 9 3 6	7 7 2 9 6

(*continued on next page*)

Table 8—*continued*

8 4 6 8 6	2 1 9 9 7	2 2 1 8 9	5 1 9 2 4	5 2 6 2 8	1 6 8 8 3	8 1 9 4 1
9 9 4 5 8	4 4 8 7 8	8 7 5 9 7	3 6 4 7 7	3 8 5 3 6	4 4 6 7 7	6 6 8 7 8
6 6 3 1 1	6 8 3 1 9	7 5 7 5 5	6 5 1 8 5	2 4 3 8 2	5 1 4 3 6	4 9 7 8 6
7 3 7 7 2	7 3 6 2 2	3 8 9 4 6	4 7 2 6 9	7 9 7 4 1	3 8 2 6 5	3 5 3 1 4
2 8 9 3 4	1 5 5 5 1	5 4 3 6 4	7 8 7 5 3	9 5 8 6 5	8 2 7 9 2	5 3 4 3 5
3 7 2 6 9	8 6 4 6 3	4 1 8 2 1	1 9 6 4 8	4 7 2 1 3	6 3 5 5 1	2 2 6 9 9
5 1 8 4 5	9 9 1 8 4	1 9 4 3 2	8 2 8 9 6	6 3 4 9 9	2 7 1 2 4	9 8 2 6 2
4 5 5 2 7	3 2 7 3 6	9 3 2 1 8	9 3 5 1 2	1 6 9 7 7	9 5 9 1 8	7 7 1 5 7
1 2 1 9 3	5 7 2 4 5	6 6 6 7 3	2 4 3 3 1	8 1 1 5 4	7 9 3 4 9	1 4 5 2 3
8 6 2 2 4	5 4 5 8 3	9 6 5 2 2	4 9 8 2 9	8 6 6 5 6	3 5 6 6 5	1 1 3 9 1
2 2 3 3 9	8 1 8 3 7	6 5 1 3 8	3 6 9 1 6	3 7 4 3 5	9 3 2 5 2	5 8 1 3 5
7 5 6 9 5	4 2 6 6 1	7 4 4 9 6	1 3 3 7 5	9 4 8 8 8	5 4 1 8 7	2 2 8 8 2
5 4 4 5 3	7 5 2 2 4	5 9 9 8 4	5 8 5 9 4	6 1 2 7 7	1 1 5 4 9	4 4 5 7 9
6 8 1 8 2	9 6 1 4 5	4 7 8 6 9	7 4 2 8 2	2 5 5 4 4	4 8 8 1 3	9 7 6 6 8
1 9 9 1 1	3 9 4 1 9	3 3 3 7 5	6 5 1 4 1	4 8 9 1 1	2 9 9 3 8	8 6 2 5 7
9 1 8 4 8	1 7 9 7 6	2 1 7 4 3	8 2 7 3 7	7 9 1 6 9	6 6 4 2 6	6 5 7 2 4
3 3 5 6 6	2 8 7 5 2	8 2 6 1 7	2 7 4 6 3	5 3 7 9 2	8 7 7 9 1	3 3 4 1 3
4 7 7 7 7	6 3 3 9 8	1 8 2 5 1	9 1 6 5 8	1 2 3 2 3	7 2 3 7 4	7 9 9 4 6
6 5 3 4 8	9 5 3 8 2	1 6 4 4 6	8 4 9 9 1	4 3 3 7 9	9 3 4 5 9	3 2 5 6 1
2 3 7 5 9	6 1 7 5 4	8 4 5 9 1	3 7 1 8 5	7 1 9 1 3	6 9 8 1 5	6 4 4 9 2
7 4 9 8 2	4 7 2 1 9	6 7 2 8 7	5 5 6 6 2	8 8 4 3 7	2 5 7 3 1	5 5 3 2 5
5 2 2 9 6	7 2 5 9 5	3 2 6 1 8	6 2 4 3 9	6 5 6 2 1	3 4 5 6 3	9 3 2 4 4
4 7 5 1 7	2 9 8 6 8	5 9 9 2 5	9 3 2 2 8	2 9 2 4 8	4 2 6 4 2	7 9 7 5 6
8 9 4 3 3	3 6 1 2 7	2 8 8 6 9	4 8 7 7 4	1 2 5 9 4	7 6 1 2 7	2 8 6 7 3
1 1 6 2 1	8 4 6 4 1	9 1 1 3 2	2 1 8 5 7	3 7 8 6 2	5 8 2 9 6	4 7 1 3 7
3 8 1 6 4	1 3 9 3 3	7 5 3 5 4	1 9 3 1 6	5 6 1 5 5	8 7 3 8 4	1 1 9 1 8
9 6 8 7 5	5 8 4 7 6	4 3 7 7 3	7 6 5 4 3	9 4 7 8 6	1 1 9 7 8	8 6 8 8 9
7 4 2 4 2	1 2 2 6 2	8 6 5 2 2	6 1 8 4 7	1 2 1 8 3	9 7 7 4 5	4 6 1 4 7
8 5 9 8 7	8 3 9 2 3	1 1 6 5 9	7 7 2 9 3	5 4 4 7 8	3 4 1 1 7	6 5 8 1 6
9 6 4 5 9	3 1 3 7 5	7 4 2 8 8	9 9 4 5 8	2 9 6 1 7	4 6 3 3 6	9 8 3 7 8
1 7 7 6 3	6 6 7 4 8	9 7 1 6 7	1 5 7 8 5	6 5 2 4 6	6 2 5 9 8	1 4 5 9 2
2 2 8 7 5	5 9 1 5 9	5 5 9 4 6	2 3 3 6 4	7 6 5 3 4	2 5 6 7 4	7 1 9 5 4
5 9 1 2 1	4 8 5 1 6	6 9 3 9 4	3 4 9 2 9	9 1 9 2 1	7 9 2 6 1	3 3 2 2 9
6 3 6 1 6	7 7 8 9 4	3 8 4 1 3	5 6 5 1 1	8 8 8 9 2	5 3 4 5 2	5 7 7 8 5
4 1 5 9 8	2 5 4 3 7	4 3 8 3 5	8 2 6 3 6	4 7 7 6 9	8 8 9 2 3	2 2 4 6 1
3 8 3 3 4	9 4 6 8 1	2 2 7 7 1	4 8 1 7 2	3 3 3 5 5	1 1 8 8 9	8 9 6 3 3

(*continued on next page*)

Table 8—*continued*

```
97597  32358  11761  22663  73827  41767  89437
25775  26672  27813  48859  81989  79388  92192
72339  51744  53276  73232  38665  83826  56281
44852  49519  82455  99945  14346  95693  78849
53988  15296  64594  55577  96291  68442  37768
66146  93127  48942  67128  47773  54939  11615
39464  74935  99628  31784  62554  16174  44926
88221  67863  76187  86491  29418  37551  23374
11613  88481  35339  14316  55132  22215  65553

25665  42832  48626  42413  98197  47496  13414
81157  65718  77278  31168  37265  85672  41959
49239  36666  34347  58235  81671  32824  32873
78481  94493  56835  19396  62832  53169  54765
54572  23945  99482  93549  16344  64948  25341
32396  18177  65169  75624  76488  11583  67136
16923  57329  23711  67771  53556  98331  76698
63718  89284  11993  24957  24929  26217  95827

97844  71551  82554  86882  49413  79755  89282
98119  47634  62128  74824  26316  69967  99242
42293  62781  39637  56945  93661  35153  26837
71926  19563  58873  41611  12194  24228  17798
17455  58857  11764  19452  57975  47815  52523
66834  25245  27285  25299  71782  88679  34114
29662  83196  93516  32777  64843  92581  73375
35341  74918  44949  93188  85428  71742  68486
84787  96479  76491  68563  38259  16396  81659
53578  31322  85352  87336  49537  53434  45961

24814  99952  56378  32381  21148  97297  72848
52498  87383  22131  69919  15466  36866  98794
71675  78536  73495  27778  77622  55159  51263
98581  33164  49769  86257  88255  72928  85426
37137  45775  97913  51435  93913  14312  16975
63226  16691  38586  93122  54874  29581  44112
86349  64849  61622  15644  62331  63645  39681
19752  22217  85847  48893  46597  48774  63557
45963  51428  14254  74566  39789  81433  27339
```

(*continued on next page*)

Table 8—*continued*

---

3 5 9 5 1	4 1 8 8 6	6 5 4 5 5	3 9 8 6 3	8 6 8 9 1	2 6 5 3 1	1 2 7 7 2
6 2 7 3 7	2 8 6 2 2	9 7 7 7 4	9 4 3 9 9	6 5 6 1 5	7 1 3 8 5	3 6 3 9 6
9 3 2 8 9	5 3 4 9 1	2 1 3 9 7	1 6 2 1 2	9 8 5 3 2	1 2 4 6 3	8 3 5 2 7
5 7 6 9 3	7 5 7 4 3	4 9 6 6 1	7 7 7 4 7	5 4 3 5 8	4 4 1 2 4	5 9 2 1 3
7 4 8 6 2	8 7 5 1 5	5 4 2 4 6	4 3 5 8 5	1 9 7 7 9	8 7 8 5 9	6 4 9 5 9
1 9 1 7 4	3 9 2 5 9	3 3 1 1 3	8 2 1 5 1	4 7 9 2 4	5 9 6 4 2	7 5 8 3 4
8 6 5 1 8	6 6 1 6 8	1 2 8 3 8	2 5 9 7 4	3 1 1 4 7	9 3 9 9 8	4 1 1 4 1
4 8 4 2 6	1 4 9 3 7	8 8 5 2 2	6 8 6 2 8	7 3 4 8 3	3 8 2 1 7	9 7 4 6 8
2 1 3 4 5	9 2 3 7 4	7 6 9 8 9	5 1 4 3 6	2 2 2 6 6	6 5 7 7 6	2 8 6 8 5
4 6 6 2 2	2 2 5 6 5	5 7 5 6 4	6 2 7 1 6	4 8 3 4 6	2 2 5 7 5	7 6 3 5 6
3 2 2 3 4	7 7 9 7 9	6 1 2 9 1	1 9 1 4 3	1 9 2 2 2	9 8 3 1 3	5 4 1 2 7
2 5 5 5 3	6 6 1 2 7	8 9 6 5 6	4 7 9 3 1	8 4 5 7 7	4 6 7 8 1	4 3 7 1 8
1 4 8 7 1	3 3 8 1 3	4 8 8 7 9	3 3 2 2 9	3 7 7 6 9	7 9 6 9 8	3 8 5 9 9
9 1 4 8 5	9 8 3 8 4	2 3 4 4 8	7 5 5 8 2	9 5 1 1 8	6 7 8 6 2	8 2 8 6 5
5 7 9 9 7	1 5 6 5 6	3 6 1 8 5	5 6 8 6 4	2 1 8 8 4	5 3 9 4 6	6 1 4 8 4
7 8 3 6 6	8 4 2 9 2	7 4 7 2 2	2 8 6 5 7	7 6 6 9 3	8 4 1 3 7	9 9 6 3 2
6 3 1 4 8	4 9 4 3 8	1 5 9 3 7	8 1 4 9 8	5 2 4 5 5	3 1 2 2 9	1 7 2 7 3
8 9 7 1 9	5 1 7 4 1	9 2 3 1 3	9 4 3 7 5	6 3 9 3 1	1 5 4 5 4	2 5 9 4 1
8 5 3 9 2	1 7 9 9 6	5 8 8 8 5	3 8 2 4 7	8 4 1 3 8	7 1 1 6 5	4 4 7 2 2
7 2 5 7 5	9 9 4 7 7	9 1 1 1 7	9 3 8 5 6	7 7 3 4 7	8 2 8 7 5	2 9 1 4 7
5 1 4 5 7	7 2 3 4 1	7 2 3 9 4	4 7 9 1 9	6 2 5 1 9	3 4 7 3 1	8 2 8 9 8
9 6 7 2 4	4 6 8 1 5	2 3 9 3 1	7 5 7 8 5	9 5 7 9 4	1 5 9 2 3	5 7 2 1 3
4 8 6 8 3	2 8 6 2 4	4 6 5 7 8	5 2 1 6 8	1 1 9 8 3	9 9 4 8 8	6 1 5 8 6
6 4 9 6 8	5 1 1 8 3	6 4 7 6 3	1 9 3 3 2	3 3 6 2 2	2 7 2 9 9	7 3 3 5 5
2 7 8 4 6	6 4 5 6 9	8 5 2 5 6	8 1 4 7 1	4 9 4 6 1	5 8 6 1 7	9 5 6 3 4
1 9 2 1 1	3 5 2 3 2	1 9 4 4 9	2 6 6 2 4	5 8 2 5 6	6 6 3 5 6	1 8 4 6 1
3 3 1 3 9	8 3 7 5 8	3 7 6 2 2	6 4 5 9 3	2 6 8 7 5	4 3 5 4 4	6 3 9 7 9
7 3 6 5 3	3 2 8 9 6	3 1 4 6 8	8 4 6 8 6	6 3 7 1 2	5 8 5 3 5	1 8 4 7 5
5 5 4 2 6	9 1 5 3 7	2 2 2 7 4	6 6 3 6 4	7 8 3 6 8	9 4 9 7 9	7 2 9 5 7
4 8 8 1 5	4 9 7 5 9	1 6 9 1 2	2 9 1 9 9	4 6 2 9 3	8 7 4 2 8	9 4 5 2 3
3 7 3 4 8	5 5 1 2 1	8 8 5 5 9	5 1 5 2 2	3 7 5 7 4	6 1 1 1 4	5 7 8 4 8
8 9 5 9 7	1 4 9 1 2	6 4 6 8 7	3 3 9 7 1	5 9 1 5 5	1 3 6 4 6	3 3 6 3 9
2 6 9 8 1	2 8 3 6 3	4 7 8 2 1	4 8 4 1 3	1 4 4 3 7	7 9 2 8 7	4 9 2 6 1
6 4 2 3 2	7 7 6 8 5	5 3 3 9 3	7 2 2 3 5	8 2 9 4 6	3 2 3 6 2	6 5 1 9 4
9 1 1 7 9	6 3 4 4 8	9 5 7 4 5	1 5 8 5 8	2 1 8 2 9	2 6 7 5 1	2 6 3 8 2
1 2 7 6 4	8 6 2 7 4	7 9 1 3 6	9 7 7 4 7	9 5 6 8 1	4 5 8 9 3	8 1 7 1 6

(*continued on next page*)

Table 8—*continued*

4 7 7 1 2	4 4 4 2 9	8 7 4 5 5	7 1 1 9 1	2 2 4 1 7	8 8 2 7 1	4 7 6 9 8
9 4 2 2 4	2 1 6 6 4	5 2 3 3 7	4 3 5 8 9	9 7 7 9 3	2 6 8 4 8	8 9 1 8 1
3 1 8 3 6	5 3 9 8 8	4 3 1 7 8	8 4 2 6 8	7 5 8 3 8	4 5 7 9 2	7 4 7 5 2
1 8 3 4 7	8 7 2 3 1	9 5 8 2 3	2 5 3 7 4	3 9 9 5 6	5 3 1 3 4	5 3 5 2 3
5 3 9 9 8	9 6 5 9 6	2 8 2 4 4	1 7 8 4 2	5 8 6 8 4	6 2 5 6 6	2 2 9 1 4
6 2 5 7 1	6 8 8 4 7	3 1 6 9 6	9 6 9 2 7	8 6 5 4 9	9 4 9 5 5	9 5 2 6 9
2 6 1 8 9	3 5 3 5 3	7 4 7 1 2	3 8 6 3 6	4 4 1 6 1	7 9 3 1 9	6 8 4 7 5
7 9 6 5 5	7 2 1 1 2	6 9 5 6 1	5 9 4 1 3	6 1 3 7 5	3 7 6 8 7	1 6 3 3 6
8 5 4 6 3	1 9 7 7 5	1 6 9 8 9	6 2 7 5 5	1 3 2 2 2	1 1 4 2 3	3 1 8 4 7
7 4 7 8 5	3 5 9 5 7	6 7 4 1 3	2 2 2 8 4	4 2 2 2 5	4 4 4 1 7	1 1 5 1 7
1 7 5 4 6	5 4 1 7 6	8 8 3 8 5	5 1 9 5 6	3 7 7 5 1	5 8 6 9 4	8 5 1 3 3
2 6 1 1 9	8 8 8 3 3	2 6 5 9 6	9 5 8 4 5	6 4 6 8 3	1 9 7 2 1	4 3 2 6 4
6 3 6 2 7	7 7 4 1 5	9 3 1 3 1	3 3 1 7 1	9 5 1 3 7	9 5 9 5 3	6 9 8 5 6
3 5 4 9 8	2 6 6 6 9	4 2 9 5 7	6 7 7 3 7	5 6 3 9 2	6 3 2 7 2	5 8 7 9 1
4 8 9 6 2	9 9 7 8 2	3 9 7 7 9	1 6 5 9 9	2 1 5 6 9	8 1 1 6 8	3 7 6 2 5
9 1 2 5 1	4 1 2 4 1	7 4 6 4 4	4 8 4 1 3	1 3 4 4 6	2 2 5 3 6	2 2 4 8 8
5 2 8 3 4	6 2 3 2 8	5 1 2 2 2	8 4 6 6 2	7 8 8 7 4	3 7 3 4 9	9 4 3 7 9
8 9 3 7 3	1 3 5 9 4	1 5 8 6 8	7 9 3 2 8	8 9 9 1 8	7 6 8 8 5	7 6 9 4 2
1 1 2 8 9	7 2 1 6 1	9 1 1 4 2	7 1 6 4 4	6 1 9 9 1	7 9 2 2 5	6 1 9 4 9
6 7 1 5 3	4 9 6 4 4	8 4 6 8 7	9 2 4 2 6	9 5 2 2 2	6 3 3 5 9	5 5 2 6 1
7 3 9 7 5	5 6 7 8 6	3 5 8 7 5	5 9 9 6 2	4 9 6 7 6	4 6 1 6 1	4 4 8 5 2
3 9 5 1 2	3 1 2 5 9	6 6 7 3 1	8 6 5 5 3	7 4 5 5 9	5 7 7 8 7	3 7 4 7 5
5 4 4 9 1	2 8 5 3 2	2 3 2 2 4	1 4 1 8 5	3 6 7 3 3	3 4 8 1 6	2 9 1 9 8
8 5 8 3 6	1 5 9 7 7	5 2 5 1 9	3 8 7 1 8	8 3 8 1 8	1 5 4 4 4	9 3 3 3 6
9 2 7 6 8	8 3 8 2 8	1 9 3 9 8	4 5 2 9 7	5 8 1 6 4	2 1 5 9 3	8 2 7 2 3
4 6 3 4 4	6 4 3 1 3	4 7 4 5 3	6 3 3 3 9	2 7 3 4 5	8 8 9 3 8	7 6 5 8 7
2 8 6 2 7	9 7 4 9 5	7 8 9 6 6	2 7 8 7 1	1 2 4 8 7	9 2 6 7 2	1 8 6 1 4
3 7 4 1 5	5 3 6 9 8	8 7 6 4 4	1 7 9 6 6	7 1 8 3 3	3 3 7 1 6	8 9 5 2 5
7 8 9 6 2	2 1 3 6 5	9 6 2 2 2	7 1 4 5 9	9 3 2 1 1	2 7 5 6 5	6 2 9 4 9
2 4 6 4 9	4 5 4 8 6	6 3 3 1 6	9 5 1 1 1	2 9 7 6 5	1 9 3 4 8	5 5 1 1 7
4 6 5 3 6	1 9 5 3 3	3 2 7 6 7	2 4 3 4 8	1 6 1 4 9	7 6 8 9 3	9 3 2 8 1
1 2 7 7 1	3 4 9 5 1	7 5 9 7 1	5 6 7 7 5	5 4 6 2 7	4 5 9 7 9	2 1 8 7 2
5 9 8 9 7	7 3 1 1 7	5 9 1 8 5	3 3 8 8 2	6 8 9 5 4	8 8 1 2 4	1 8 4 9 8
6 5 3 2 3	9 7 7 7 2	4 8 4 3 8	6 2 5 3 7	3 7 4 7 8	6 2 3 5 7	7 6 6 6 6
9 1 1 8 4	8 8 8 2 9	2 4 5 9 9	4 8 2 2 3	8 2 3 9 6	5 1 4 3 2	4 7 3 3 3
8 3 2 5 8	6 6 2 4 4	1 1 8 5 3	8 9 6 9 4	4 5 5 8 2	9 4 2 8 1	3 4 7 5 4

Source: Reprinted, by permission, from W. G. Cochran and G. M. Cox, *Experimental Designs* (New York: John Wiley & Sons, 1950).

Table 9. Random orderings of numbers 1–16.

7	12	15	15	1	2	7	16	10	2	14	15	7	13	13	10	6	1	8	10
13	3	8	16	7	10	11	10	13	5	11	7	13	16	7	7	5	13	2	14
3	1	4	5	14	13	3	14	9	13	13	2	9	15	6	2	8	4	5	8
11	8	16	14	15	6	2	6	2	16	8	5	12	3	9	13	4	3	10	4
14	9	1	6	3	9	14	13	8	6	5	8	14	7	3	15	13	11	4	7
2	16	10	13	5	5	13	2	11	7	3	12	5	14	12	16	2	2	9	15
4	6	13	7	2	15	1	9	1	4	7	10	6	9	11	9	7	6	16	11
6	14	6	10	4	14	4	15	3	3	4	16	2	6	5	1	12	10	6	9
10	15	2	1	13	12	16	3	4	8	10	1	15	5	14	12	14	12	3	2
12	10	7	12	9	11	9	8	12	14	15	4	11	8	16	8	9	14	14	1
15	7	5	2	10	7	8	12	6	15	6	13	16	12	15	4	11	8	12	6
16	2	11	8	8	8	15	5	16	1	1	9	8	1	8	14	16	5	13	5
9	13	14	3	6	4	10	11	5	12	9	3	10	4	4	3	10	9	1	3
8	11	9	4	11	3	12	7	7	10	12	14	3	10	1	6	15	16	15	12
1	5	12	11	16	16	5	4	14	9	16	11	1	2	10	5	1	15	7	13
5	4	3	9	12	1	6	1	15	11	2	6	4	11	2	11	3	7	11	16
11	8	16	5	5	13	1	13	2	16	14	12	9	8	7	5	13	3	13	3
2	2	8	8	14	16	4	3	8	11	10	14	15	1	2	11	4	5	15	9
6	13	2	13	6	5	9	15	11	10	12	6	16	15	16	9	10	12	16	15
14	12	4	16	16	11	14	10	5	12	3	3	12	14	15	13	6	4	1	16
8	6	3	9	4	10	6	4	16	2	2	9	8	16	4	6	5	15	7	8
9	15	12	10	3	2	12	6	1	15	4	13	7	7	9	12	14	8	8	11
3	10	11	12	13	12	5	11	7	8	9	5	14	11	10	1	3	13	3	5
16	1	13	14	8	14	15	5	3	7	11	15	6	12	5	7	11	1	14	4
1	14	14	2	9	15	16	14	6	14	7	8	3	13	11	8	7	7	12	7
4	4	6	4	12	3	11	8	15	9	8	1	13	6	3	3	15	9	9	12
15	5	1	11	10	6	3	7	10	5	5	11	10	10	12	15	16	14	5	2
5	3	5	6	7	7	13	2	14	3	16	4	5	5	13	4	9	16	2	6
12	7	15	15	15	9	8	12	12	13	15	10	1	4	6	16	2	6	11	1
10	11	10	3	2	4	2	1	4	6	6	7	11	9	14	10	8	11	4	13
7	9	7	7	11	1	7	16	13	1	13	2	4	2	1	2	12	2	10	14
13	16	9	1	1	8	10	9	9	4	1	16	2	3	8	14	1	10	6	10
1	6	7	4	8	6	5	2	8	15	4	6	6	1	4	5	7	13	2	10
9	15	11	3	11	15	9	10	1	3	8	2	15	7	9	8	16	1	14	3
10	16	4	5	12	9	16	11	7	1	7	16	11	8	3	3	12	2	3	4
4	14	1	9	5	5	4	13	6	8	15	5	12	5	7	16	5	11	8	1

(continued on next page)

Table 9—*continued*

7	3	13	14	15	2	1	14	16	5	14	9	2	16	1	12	6	14	4	13
16	11	2	1	14	16	6	9	3	4	16	14	3	15	11	11	3	9	12	5
3	10	16	16	13	7	13	1	11	14	9	10	16	2	10	2	10	7	10	16
11	13	9	13	4	13	8	3	5	13	10	12	5	12	5	14	13	16	5	6
15	2	3	12	9	12	2	4	13	10	3	13	14	4	2	1	14	8	6	12
14	1	14	6	10	1	3	12	4	2	2	4	13	3	16	9	9	3	7	14
13	12	5	11	3	11	15	8	2	7	11	7	8	14	6	4	4	4	15	11
12	5	10	7	2	14	7	15	14	16	13	1	9	10	12	10	11	10	9	8
8	9	8	10	6	4	11	7	10	11	6	8	4	9	8	15	8	6	11	9
2	7	6	2	1	8	10	6	15	12	1	11	7	11	13	6	1	15	13	15
6	4	15	8	16	10	14	16	9	6	12	3	10	6	14	7	2	12	16	7
5	8	12	15	7	3	12	5	12	9	5	15	1	13	15	13	15	5	1	2
13	4	10	4	16	13	16	13	5	3	6	14	1	16	8	7	2	3	3	12
5	14	4	6	8	2	15	1	13	14	16	4	15	4	3	12	12	1	4	7
2	2	2	15	14	16	9	12	16	6	10	15	14	9	10	1	14	8	8	16
7	12	15	8	12	3	5	14	7	12	5	13	16	1	7	5	11	2	9	3
6	9	7	14	9	14	10	11	15	11	12	1	12	12	14	16	3	11	11	8
14	5	16	7	10	8	11	8	14	13	7	11	6	3	11	4	4	6	6	9
15	11	8	9	7	12	8	7	1	15	9	3	3	7	13	11	10	4	5	1
11	6	6	1	4	1	3	16	12	5	4	9	13	13	6	8	15	9	1	14
4	10	3	16	2	11	7	9	6	9	1	8	4	11	5	2	16	10	12	4
1	8	1	13	1	15	4	4	11	4	2	16	5	8	1	9	5	12	16	6
9	7	14	2	6	4	14	10	9	8	15	10	7	10	9	10	6	14	10	11
12	1	9	10	15	5	2	15	10	2	14	2	8	2	4	13	8	5	15	5
3	3	12	11	5	9	6	6	3	10	13	12	9	6	2	15	7	15	7	13
10	15	11	5	13	7	12	5	2	7	11	5	10	15	12	3	1	13	13	10
8	13	13	3	3	10	13	2	4	1	8	6	11	14	15	6	9	16	2	2
16	16	5	12	11	6	1	3	8	16	3	7	2	5	16	14	13	7	14	15
9	16	15	12	2	11	4	16	11	10	2	5	5	14	11	2	14	13	16	6
11	3	2	6	15	13	10	1	4	13	11	8	16	16	4	3	5	15	5	15
14	14	8	16	11	15	5	14	14	11	1	14	15	15	13	5	7	11	11	16
4	13	1	3	5	7	6	2	16	1	14	9	14	3	3	1	6	16	6	10
6	6	10	7	13	10	16	7	2	12	6	12	6	13	8	9	15	9	1	11
2	10	14	9	12	3	3	10	5	6	5	16	12	10	15	10	11	4	9	8
5	15	11	14	10	4	14	13	6	4	12	4	11	5	10	14	16	5	7	9

(*continued on next page*)

Table 9—*continued*

16	5	13	10	3		9	12	6	3	7		3	7	3	11	14		7	3	14	4	12
8	12	7	11	7		8	13	15	13	9		4	3	8	1	12		6	9	8	15	14
1	8	3	2	1		5	15	9	9	3		10	11	13	8	5		13	12	3	3	5
13	9	9	1	6		2	11	3	8	8		15	1	7	9	7		8	8	6	2	3
15	1	5	5	9		6	9	4	10	5		8	13	10	7	9		15	2	10	8	4
7	4	12	13	16		1	2	11	12	2		16	15	2	4	2		11	1	7	13	1
10	2	4	15	4		16	1	12	7	15		9	10	9	12	16		4	13	2	10	13
3	7	6	8	8		14	7	5	1	14		13	2	4	2	1		16	4	1	12	7
12	11	16	4	14		12	8	8	15	16		7	6	1	6	6		12	10	12	14	2
12	6	13	4	5		7	2	1	9	2		5	1	15	2	14		13	13	11	2	13
6	11	4	15	12		12	6	15	6	15		6	3	12	5	15		11	16	9	8	1
13	5	1	6	7		6	13	5	7	8		15	6	4	15	1		14	5	14	10	4
11	1	11	7	8		15	8	4	12	13		16	9	3	10	7		2	12	3	9	8
3	7	3	14	15		4	12	11	4	10		8	12	1	4	16		6	2	2	16	7
10	12	15	11	4		13	5	10	3	14		11	2	9	11	2		9	9	12	12	11
15	9	16	16	9		2	16	2	15	6		7	15	8	1	8		12	4	13	6	9
14	15	2	13	3		16	10	14	13	9		10	7	14	9	6		5	6	4	11	12
1	2	12	9	1		8	15	3	8	11		2	5	10	3	3		10	10	7	13	10
5	10	5	3	13		9	9	13	10	1		3	8	7	8	9		4	15	15	7	15
7	14	9	2	11		14	11	6	14	12		9	10	16	12	13		3	7	5	4	14
9	8	10	1	6		3	3	8	5	6		14	16	2	7	12		16	14	10	15	5
2	3	7	5	10		1	1	12	2	7		1	4	6	16	10		8	8	1	5	16
16	13	14	10	2		5	7	16	1	16		13	11	11	6	5		1	11	16	3	3
4	4	6	8	14		10	14	7	11	3		4	13	13	13	11		15	3	6	14	6
8	16	8	12	16		11	4	9	16	4		12	14	5	14	4		7	1	8	1	2
3	14	11	8	9		14	14	2	13	1		8	4	15	16	7		6	15	13	13	13
12	9	6	9	8		10	12	13	14	5		11	10	10	12	9		10	5	16	6	3
11	11	7	1	11		13	11	4	2	7		16	5	8	3	11		12	6	12	5	11
1	16	9	3	1		7	8	15	5	4		3	7	16	8	12		15	7	5	9	4
13	3	1	2	13		5	4	9	7	6		5	15	4	6	4		1	10	6	1	14
7	12	10	10	5		15	5	8	16	2		12	3	5	13	14		13	13	2	3	7
10	15	15	4	14		1	16	16	12	11		9	16	1	2	10		11	8	7	16	8
15	7	4	14	7		4	7	10	6	10		1	1	2	11	3		16	2	4	2	1
9	5	2	7	3		3	13	14	15	15		6	12	9	15	15		9	16	15	15	10
8	6	16	5	15		8	2	12	1	3		10	8	3	14	13		2	1	10	8	12
2	10	5	11	4		9	3	6	11	12		15	9	7	5	2		8	14	1	4	5
5	4	3	15	2		2	15	11	10	14		7	14	14	7	6		3	11	11	10	2

(*continued on next page*)

Table 9—*continued*

4	1	12	12	16	6	1	3	4	16	13	11	11	4	1	7	12	3	7	9
6	13	14	6	12	16	9	1	8	8	4	13	12	10	5	5	4	9	12	16
16	8	8	13	10	11	10	5	9	13	14	2	6	9	8	14	9	14	11	15
14	2	13	16	6	12	6	7	3	9	2	6	13	1	16	4	3	8	14	6
1	2	14	12	4	4	3	6	12	7	11	11	9	13	13	7	4	10	16	9
9	3	10	13	3	5	5	13	15	9	14	13	14	9	9	4	8	4	15	2
13	6	15	10	11	3	15	12	4	5	5	4	3	6	4	5	12	14	14	3
8	5	5	15	8	9	8	8	2	3	1	12	8	3	11	2	9	16	10	12
11	12	9	14	16	11	4	15	1	4	3	15	5	15	7	11	16	15	7	1
10	4	13	6	1	13	12	9	8	6	7	8	15	7	3	8	13	9	8	10
16	11	11	16	7	15	9	5	7	2	6	10	16	10	6	1	3	6	1	13
5	7	4	3	2	1	14	2	10	13	16	1	6	4	15	6	15	12	11	16
3	15	12	2	14	8	11	16	14	16	9	7	13	8	2	16	2	11	2	15
7	9	7	9	13	6	2	4	13	14	15	6	10	11	8	12	10	3	3	8
2	10	8	8	15	14	6	3	5	1	4	3	7	2	14	15	14	2	6	4
15	8	3	1	6	2	10	7	3	10	10	2	4	1	5	3	7	13	13	14
6	13	2	5	5	7	13	10	16	15	12	16	1	14	16	14	6	1	9	7
12	16	16	4	10	10	7	1	9	8	2	5	12	16	12	9	11	7	4	5
4	1	1	7	9	12	16	11	6	11	8	14	2	5	1	10	1	5	12	6
14	14	6	11	12	6	1	14	11	12	13	9	11	12	10	13	5	8	5	11
16	2	15	13	13	2	11	14	4	3	12	11	11	11	7	4	13	7	16	16
7	10	8	2	9	5	14	15	5	16	5	9	9	3	1	2	5	6	3	5
9	16	3	8	4	8	7	2	11	1	13	15	2	5	6	8	2	11	6	10
8	11	14	11	14	7	5	7	6	9	16	4	5	16	9	9	16	4	8	15
3	15	11	14	8	10	10	10	12	10	2	2	13	1	11	11	12	13	5	3
12	7	13	15	12	3	12	8	8	11	10	12	10	7	14	15	14	10	12	4
15	13	9	3	3	14	6	16	2	13	8	14	15	14	12	7	1	1	7	13
10	4	1	4	16	6	1	12	16	15	3	16	3	6	16	6	8	3	9	11
6	1	6	5	6	1	15	11	7	8	1	1	8	9	2	16	10	14	14	2
11	8	16	16	5	13	13	6	15	2	15	5	12	8	3	10	11	8	2	14
13	9	10	1	15	15	9	9	3	14	6	6	1	10	13	13	9	5	15	1
14	5	4	6	1	12	3	4	14	6	4	10	4	4	15	3	15	2	1	12
5	12	7	12	10	11	8	3	1	4	7	8	7	15	10	5	3	9	11	7
2	3	2	10	7	4	16	5	10	5	14	13	6	12	5	12	4	16	4	9
4	14	12	7	11	16	4	13	13	12	11	3	14	2	4	14	6	15	10	8
1	6	5	9	2	9	2	1	9	7	9	7	16	13	8	1	7	12	13	6
13	4	3	11	16	8	7	16	3	16	1	10	1	15	16	10	11	4	6	4
4	1	6	16	6	11	11	14	4	8	3	3	5	3	6	7	7	8	5	12
2	7	15	5	7	7	16	3	2	7	10	8	11	11	7	16	12	15	9	9

(*continued on next page*)

Table 9—*continued*

3	8	12	10	8	6	4	4	11	10	9	2	4	7	1	3	15	10	14	11
6	15	4	6	3	10	2	12	15	6	6	16	9	4	8	12	8	2	8	6
5	6	10	2	13	15	8	7	16	3	2	12	10	9	12	14	9	5	13	5
12	11	1	13	4	5	3	15	5	12	12	1	15	5	15	6	4	12	4	14
9	9	11	8	2	3	12	9	14	13	13	6	8	6	13	11	3	1	10	7
7	13	5	7	1	14	6	13	8	11	14	5	3	16	4	13	10	13	15	3
10	2	14	14	15	16	1	2	1	9	8	15	2	14	9	1	1	7	3	13
14	16	2	1	14	9	13	5	6	4	11	13	16	12	10	15	2	9	2	16
16	3	8	9	5	1	14	6	10	1	16	9	6	10	14	5	6	6	7	15
11	10	16	12	12	12	10	1	12	14	7	14	12	8	3	4	5	16	12	8
15	5	9	15	9	13	9	11	9	5	4	4	13	2	5	8	14	3	1	1
1	12	7	3	10	2	5	10	13	15	5	7	14	1	2	2	16	11	16	2
8	14	13	4	11	4	15	8	7	2	15	11	7	13	11	9	13	14	11	10
1	4	10	3	8	16	4	10	6	10	12	13	16	6	12	10	5	12	1	10
3	10	12	5	7	11	3	3	7	1	6	1	13	2	7	12	16	10	11	13
13	15	5	1	1	12	15	12	14	4	10	14	11	12	4	15	13	16	9	3
10	5	2	9	13	2	16	9	4	2	7	7	4	10	10	6	1	9	5	9
7	6	15	14	15	15	2	7	9	15	2	16	10	8	11	14	4	3	8	15
11	1	11	8	9	7	12	11	11	5	11	3	6	4	15	1	12	4	6	1
12	3	4	2	3	3	1	13	13	12	9	11	1	3	6	2	15	14	7	4
14	9	7	16	14	1	10	16	16	6	8	15	3	16	14	16	14	2	2	7
5	12	13	4	4	14	14	4	5	7	16	5	14	14	8	5	7	15	10	12
4	13	14	13	6	6	8	14	8	9	13	10	7	7	9	3	3	13	12	6
8	14	16	12	12	13	7	2	10	13	4	12	12	5	16	9	11	6	3	16
16	7	3	10	11	9	13	5	12	16	5	9	8	9	3	13	8	8	14	11
6	2	9	15	5	8	9	8	1	11	15	6	9	13	5	11	2	11	13	5
15	8	6	6	16	4	11	1	2	8	3	4	15	15	13	7	6	5	4	14
9	11	1	7	10	5	6	6	15	4	1	2	5	11	1	8	10	1	15	8
2	16	8	11	2	10	5	15	3	3	14	8	2	1	2	4	9	7	16	2
6	12	2	3	9	14	1	16	11	14	5	7	15	11	10	14	10	16	4	16
1	2	15	9	13	15	5	12	12	9	8	6	1	2	5	1	11	13	13	15
9	7	8	13	12	7	11	13	10	5	6	13	6	5	13	9	15	4	9	10
11	1	16	1	1	5	12	4	2	10	16	4	3	16	2	8	9	8	7	7
7	14	11	5	3	4	2	15	5	12	14	9	5	10	15	5	13	9	3	4
8	11	10	10	15	12	8	11	16	13	10	10	10	3	4	12	1	3	2	11
2	4	5	6	16	16	3	2	8	4	7	11	4	7	3	2	7	14	11	1

(*continued on next page*)

Table 9—*continued*

5	9	7	8	5	6	14	7	14	1	1	2	2	15	7	4	14	15	8	8
16	5	1	11	4	8	15	5	13	8	15	16	8	9	9	11	16	12	12	3
13	10	6	12	6	11	10	6	15	15	2	3	13	1	8	10	5	10	5	12
10	3	14	4	11	3	9	1	3	11	3	14	14	6	12	3	8	1	15	5
12	15	3	14	8	9	6	14	1	6	9	15	11	4	6	7	6	2	6	6
3	16	9	15	2	1	4	3	9	16	13	1	7	13	1	16	3	11	16	13
4	8	4	2	10	10	13	9	6	7	12	8	16	8	11	15	2	6	14	2
15	13	13	16	14	2	16	8	7	3	4	5	9	4	14	13	12	5	1	14
14	6	12	7	7	13	7	10	4	2	11	12	12	12	16	6	4	7	10	9
14	15	12	8	7	4	13	14	3	10	13	14	6	3	14	8	10	13	11	14
7	1	8	11	15	11	7	2	12	15	5	8	13	5	6	13	14	2	10	13
13	9	2	15	2	13	6	5	16	3	16	7	5	15	4	7	2	12	4	10
11	3	4	6	11	16	16	4	9	7	11	1	14	9	9	12	3	10	6	2
3	16	3	13	5	1	4	6	14	6	4	3	16	8	15	11	6	1	1	15
5	12	6	9	13	2	12	10	6	1	14	16	11	12	16	3	1	7	12	1
16	5	10	10	12	5	14	15	7	12	15	2	2	10	5	9	7	6	15	7
2	4	16	12	14	3	11	1	13	14	10	6	10	11	13	14	5	15	13	4
6	6	9	3	16	6	2	12	10	13	12	5	4	14	10	15	12	5	3	8
4	7	15	14	6	14	10	9	11	8	8	15	8	13	11	2	9	8	14	12
15	14	5	7	8	10	15	8	4	2	3	11	1	6	2	16	4	4	5	5
9	13	14	4	4	9	5	3	8	9	2	4	3	4	12	5	11	16	8	6
1	2	1	2	1	7	9	11	15	16	1	13	15	12	1	10	15	3	2	9
12	11	13	1	9	8	3	7	2	11	9	9	9	7	3	1	13	11	7	11
8	8	11	16	3	12	1	13	1	5	6	12	12	16	8	6	16	14	16	16
10	10	7	5	10	15	8	16	5	4	7	10	7	1	7	4	8	9	9	3
15	1	3	2	7	5	4	11	1	11	16	13	13	12	15	8	2	7	6	11
13	16	13	7	4	16	7	9	5	1	11	11	5	14	13	5	15	15	4	12
5	14	12	11	14	4	8	7	15	13	6	16	2	1	9	3	9	14	5	6
3	15	9	3	9	11	9	8	12	6	9	14	4	2	7	11	16	5	3	15
6	11	10	9	16	14	2	10	7	14	2	6	16	3	2	4	6	11	8	1
9	2	1	16	13	6	5	5	4	5	5	4	15	16	11	12	4	2	10	7
4	7	2	12	8	1	12	12	3	9	3	15	9	5	4	14	13	8	9	9
14	3	7	4	2	13	16	2	9	7	14	10	14	13	10	2	8	12	13	5
8	12	4	10	5	2	6	1	16	10	1	12	12	9	12	15	10	4	15	2
7	4	16	8	10	9	3	15	2	3	7	2	8	7	1	7	1	1	12	10
10	9	8	13	12	3	11	6	10	8	13	1	11	6	16	10	12	13	7	4

(*continued on next page*)

Table 9—*continued*

2	13	5	1	3	15	15	3	8	2	10	5	3	15	6	13	7	3	14	3
16	10	11	15	15	7	1	16	13	12	4	9	6	8	8	9	5	9	1	13
12	5	6	14	1	12	10	14	6	15	8	7	10	10	5	16	3	10	16	16
11	6	15	6	11	10	14	4	11	16	12	8	7	11	3	1	14	16	2	8
1	8	14	5	6	8	13	13	14	4	15	3	1	4	14	6	11	6	11	14

9	16	5	1	10	2	8	1	13	11	4	14	6	7	12	15	2	8	8	1
13	7	12	16	7	9	16	12	1	14	1	9	8	10	3	16	9	11	13	13
12	8	16	2	8	8	14	4	3	2	14	7	1	16	4	3	5	13	10	11
11	6	8	7	15	13	12	11	4	10	7	2	5	3	10	8	4	2	4	3
3	11	9	3	1	1	11	14	15	9	3	1	10	8	1	9	14	12	5	8
7	12	10	8	3	15	9	7	10	8	12	8	4	11	2	2	7	6	11	6
5	2	14	14	13	14	4	13	9	7	6	5	14	2	9	7	11	15	6	9
4	5	4	15	9	4	13	6	16	4	10	15	2	5	6	10	12	16	16	7
14	1	11	5	11	5	7	5	14	12	11	10	12	15	7	4	10	5	15	15
15	4	13	4	4	6	6	3	6	5	5	4	3	1	13	12	3	10	2	2
1	13	2	6	2	3	3	2	8	6	13	12	7	9	5	11	13	3	1	10
6	10	2	12	14	11	5	10	5	13	2	11	9	14	16	14	6	14	12	4
16	9	1	10	16	7	1	9	2	16	8	6	15	12	11	13	15	9	9	5
2	14	6	13	12	12	15	8	11	3	16	16	13	6	4	5	1	1	3	12
8	3	15	9	5	16	2	15	7	15	9	13	16	4	15	1	8	4	14	14
10	15	3	11	6	10	10	16	12	1	15	3	11	13	8	6	16	7	7	16

10	7	12	15	9	16	10	8	2	2	2	12	10	4	15	3	2	6	9	5
15	5	13	8	14	12	12	15	7	9	7	2	3	16	7	16	7	8	1	14
12	10	8	3	8	5	6	14	4	4	15	3	7	7	16	6	9	9	4	15
9	15	14	2	5	3	8	10	12	8	3	7	5	5	12	8	6	13	10	10
7	2	3	4	3	14	3	3	11	11	4	4	4	6	4	2	10	2	7	3
13	13	16	10	7	1	1	7	8	13	10	1	8	14	10	1	3	12	15	12
1	3	1	6	4	15	7	6	5	15	12	5	6	2	2	10	15	10	12	2
5	14	2	12	13	2	14	13	6	5	9	10	12	3	11	12	8	1	3	9
3	8	5	1	12	9	15	1	13	10	14	16	9	13	6	7	5	5	11	7
2	1	9	5	2	8	4	4	16	7	11	9	13	15	1	15	13	11	2	11
6	9	4	7	6	10	13	5	10	14	8	15	2	8	13	5	16	4	16	16
8	16	10	9	1	6	5	2	1	3	6	8	15	11	9	9	11	7	8	4
11	6	15	16	16	13	9	11	9	12	16	6	11	9	8	13	14	16	14	1
4	4	11	11	15	11	2	16	3	16	13	11	14	12	5	11	4	14	5	13
14	12	7	13	10	4	16	12	14	6	5	13	16	1	14	4	1	15	13	6
16	11	6	14	11	7	11	9	15	1	1	14	1	10	3	14	12	3	6	8

Source: Reprinted, by permission, from W. G. Cochran and G. M. Cox, *Experimental Designs* (New York: John Wiley & Sons, 1950).

Glossary of Symbols

Symbol	Description
A, A_2, A_3	control chart factors
ACL	acceptance control limit
ANOVA	analysis of variance
AOQ	average outgoing quality
AOQL	average outgoing quality limit
APL	acceptable process level
AQL	acceptable quality level
ARL	average run length
ASN	average sample number
ATI	average total inspection
B_3, B_4, B_5, B_6	control chart factors
β_0	regression intercept
β_1	regression slope
c	count
c/n	count per unit
c_4	control chart factor
d	cell deviations
d (δ)	average of n paired differences
d_2	control chart factor
D_1, D_2, D_3, D_4	control chart factors

D	demerit
EVOP	evolutionary operation
$F(\nu_1, \nu_2)$	F-test statistic
$F(\nu_1, \nu_2, \alpha)$	critical value for F-test
$g_1(\gamma_1)$	skewness
$g_2(\gamma_2)$	kurtosis
H_0	null hypothesis
H_1	alternative hypothesis
i	cell interval
i	clearance number
LQL	limiting quality level
Med	median
MS	mean square
N	lot size
n	sample size
$np(n\pi)$	number of affected units
P_a	probability of acceptance
P_r	probability of rejection
$p(\pi)$	proportion or percent
$P_{.95}, P_{.50}$, **and so on**	measures of lot or process quality related to OC curves
p **or** p_{xy}, r **or** r_{xy}	correlation coefficient
p^2 **or** r^2	coefficient of determination
Q	quality score
R	range
RPL	rejectable process level
RQL	rejectable quality level
$s(\Sigma)$	covariance matrix
$s_d(\Sigma_d)$	covariance matrices of paired differences

s (σ)	sample standard deviation (standard deviation)
$s_{(rms)}$ ($\sigma_{(rms)}$)	sample root mean square deviation (root mean square deviation)
s^2 (σ^2)	sample variance (variance)
$s^2_{(ms)}$ ($\sigma^2_{(ms)}$)	sample mean square deviation (mean square deviation)
s_{b_0}	standard error of intercept
s_{b_1}	standard error of the slope
s_c	standard error of c
s_u	standard error of the number of counts per unit
s_p	standard error of the predicted values
s_R	standard error of the range
s_s	standard error of the sample standard deviation
$s_{\overline{X}}$	standard error of the mean
s_{xy} (σ_{xy})	covariance
$s_{\hat{Y}}$	standard error of a point on the regression line
$s_{y \cdot x}$	standard error of estimate
SS	sum of squares
source	source of variation
$T^2_{(\nu,p,\alpha)}$	central value for T^2-test
$T^2_{(\nu,p)}$	Hotelling's T^2-statistic
t_ν	t-test statistic
$t_{\nu,\alpha}$	critical value for t-test
u	count per unit
X	observed value, observation, or variate

$X\ (\mu)$	average (mean)
Y	observed value, observation, or variate
$\hat{Y}$	linear regression estimate
z	normal deviate or normal test statistic
z_α	critical value for normal test
α	significance level, risk of a type I error, producer's risk
$1 - \alpha$	confidence coefficient
β	risk of a type II error, consumer's risk
$1 - \beta$	power
X_ν^2	chi-square test statistic
$X_{\nu,\alpha}^2$	critical value for χ^2-test
ν	degrees of freedom